FALLEN ANGELS IN JEWISH, CHRISTIAN AND MOHAMMEDAN LITERATURE

BY

RABBI LEO JUNG, PH. D.

Wipf & Stock
PUBLISHERS
Eugene, Oregon

Wipf and Stock Publishers
199 W 8th Ave, Suite 3
Eugene, OR 97401

Fallen Angels in Jewish, Christian, and Mohammedan Literature
By Jung, Leo
ISBN 13: 978-1-55635-416-8
ISBN 10: 1-55635-416-9
Publication date 4/7/2007
Previously published by Dropsie College, 1926

DEDICATED TO THE MEMORY

OF MY MOTHER

THESIS APPROVED FOR THE DEGREE OF DOCTOR OF PHILOSOPHY IN THE UNIVERSITY OF LONDON.

TABLE OF CONTENTS

	Page
Foreword	vii
Preface	viii
Introduction	1
Chapter 1. THE NATURE OF ANGELS	12
Chapter 2. THE TWO SATANS	23
Chapter 3. SATAN	37
Chapter 4. OBJECTION TO THE CREATION OF MAN	45
Chapter 5. THE FALL OF MAN	68
Chapter 6. ASHMEDAI	81
Chapter 7. THE FALL OF THE ANGELS	90
Appendices	140
Literature	163
Index	169

FOREWORD

The present study on "Fallen Angels" is reprinted with revision and additions from the *Jewish Quarterly Review*. It was deemed advisable to put it in book form because of the importance of the subject alike to theologians, students of folk lore and students of English literature. As far as I am aware, this is the first exhaustive study of the subject which has been made in this department of research and the book, moreover, contains some important excursions into by-paths of the main topic. Much light has been shed upon the Lucifer legend and new matter for the date and composition of the Zohar is brought forward. It is clearly shown that the Church Fathers borrowed not only the material but also the very method of the Agadah. Theologians will find much in these pages to throw light upon such matters as the origin of sin, dualism and monotheism and the popular notions of the Satan in the Hebrew Bible as compared with the devil in the New Testament will have to be revised.

In order to fit himself for this study and not be obliged to rely upon second-hand material, the author went to the trouble of studying Persian and Anglo-Saxon—an indication of the thoroughness of his method.

It is rare that a scientific investigation appeals to such different groups of students and I venture to express the hope that the author will receive such recognition from scholars as will encourage him to continue his researches.

CYRUS ADLER.

October 25, 1926.

PREFACE

The first part of the present volume through Chapter 4 was accepted by Cambridge University, as filling the requirements for its Research Degree. The author later re-wrote those chapters, and added the other four and the appendices. The complete book was awarded the Ph.D. degree of London University. Yet the present work is only the first part of a more ambitious research which the author is following up. He hopes to complete the second part within the next three years. This will extend up to Milton's "Paradise Lost." The third part is to advance the work so that it may include examination of the sources and discussion, of "The Story of Fallen Angels in the Literature of the World," from Genesis to Anatole France.

The author desires to express his gratitude for many valuable suggestions to Professor Adolph Büchler and Dr. Moses Gaster of London, his teachers Professor A. A. Bevan and Dr. Norman McLean, and to Dr. Edward J. Thomas of Cambridge University. Dr. Cyrus Adler's courtesy and helpfulness are herewith gratefully recorded.

The thesis arose out of a doctor's dissertation on The Idea of God among the Anglo-Saxons, written in the spring of 1914 for the philosophical faculty of the University of Giessen.

In conclusion, the author wishes to acknowledge the debt he owes to the instruction and guidance of his sainted father, Dr. Meir Jung, the late Chief Rabbi of the Federation of Synagogues in London, England.

New York, September 21, 1926.   L. J.

FALLEN ANGELS IN JEWISH, CHRISTIAN AND MOHAMMEDAN LITERATURE

A Study in Comparative Folk-lore

Introduction

Haggadah: Jewish, Christian and Mohammedan

A. Jewish

Dealing as we are with legends, stories and accounts of angels, demons and all kinds of spirits, as they appear in the literature of the Rabbis and among Christian Fathers and Mohammedan sages, it will not be superfluous to digress on an examination of the position and authority of such sources in the religion and consciousness of their respective peoples. We begin with the Haggadah of the Talmud. The Talmud contains:

(1) Halakah, the discussions of Jewish laws and their results. Any such result is binding for the traditional Jew. These halakot extend and develop with the variety and increase of new conditions. In all such cases the principle which decided the more primitive case is applied to the new situation.

(2) The Haggadah, which has rightly been termed "religious folklore". It contains stories, parables, maxims, interpretations, grown neither out of a system, nor due to any definite method, but originating from the occasion of the Rabbi's sermon or from his imagination which embellished the characters of biblical stories, or

from his desire to comfort an afflicted congregation, or to arouse a new interest in their sacred lore. To give just a few telling instances:[1] Rabbi Akiba, to cheer his downhearted congregation, speaks of the virtues of Sarah, her kindness and purity, that she lived 127 years, as innocent and youthful at the end of her life as when she entered this world. The audience is not interested. Then suddenly "127" suggests to him that Queen Esther reigned over 127 provinces and he excites their interest by asking: "What caused Esther to reign over 127 provinces?"—"It is the fact that she was a descendant of Sarah who lived 127 years." The meaning underlying this is obvious. The great qualities of her ancestress which Esther inherited, eminently fitted her for the post. Esther lived in the hearts of the people as a patriotic selfless woman, and the moral of the story was both clear and impressive.

"What is the meaning of Shaddai?" asks a Rabbi on another occasion.[2] The etymology of this word was quite clear to him. He knew the text (Isaiah 13, 6) כשד משדי יבוא, and also that שדי was derived from שדד. But in telling his audience about the meaning of Shaddai (Almighty) he looked for a point which would immediately illustrate it. And thus he came to explain: "The omnipotence of God is nowhere seen so clearly as in the fact that He gave His universe a fixed law according to which all change and action should take place. He said to His world, 'Enough!', arresting its development, its laws and its forms at a definite point. Now to remind yourself without delay of what Shaddai means, think of שאמר די, Who said 'Enough, no further!'"—Most cases of "Al-tikre" serve as mnemotechnic devices. (Compare the very instructive essay on "Die Al-Tikri Deutungen" by A. Rosenzweig, in *Festschrift zu J. Levy's 70sten*

[1] Esther Rabba I.
[2] Babli Ḥagigah 12a.

Geburtstag, p. 204ff.). In a manner similar to the above, *Al-tikre* inculcates a teaching, moral or ritual, by "misreading" a word in a sentence, e. g.[3] "One should say a hundred blessings every day." That is a postulate or devout wish of some authority. To impress this fact on your mind remember the sentence, Deut. 10, 12, מה אדני אלהיך שואל ממך, "What doth the Lord thy God require of thee", but *do not read* מה, "what" the Lord thy God asks of thee, read instead מאה "a hundred" the Lord thy God asks of thee.

A moral:[4] Isaiah 54.13 ורב שלום בניך, "And great will be the peace of thy children". Do not read בניך, "thy children", read בוניך "those who build thee up."

There are innumerable sentences and interpretations of this kind. In every case the "change" is due to the idea underlying it. Hence such interpretations or translations must not be mistaken for philological truth. Yet that is exactly what happens. But none would have been more astonished than the Rabbis on hearing that their mnemotechnical devices were taken as fullblown philology.

Similar observations are necessary when we read the stories embedded in the rivers of Haggadah. Here again the purpose in telling them was to amuse, to cheer up, to let the people forget their present suffering by either leading them back to the glorious past or by painting in bright colors the fulness of time when there will be no enemy, no slander, no prejudice. There is no trace of a definite method, of any endeavor to weave these stories into a dogmatic texture, the Haggadah containing all that had occupied the popular mind, what they had heard in the beth hammidrash, or at a social gathering. Stories contradicting each other, theories incompatible with one

[3] Babli Menaḥot 43b.
[4] Babli Berakot 64a.

another, are very frequent. They are recorded as the fruits of Israel's genius. They have no authority, they form no part of Jewish religious belief. Nor may they be taken literally: it is always the idea, the lesson, and not the story, which is important. It is wrong to say that the Haggadah contains the doctrines of the Rabbis, or that only orthodox views have been admitted to the exclusion of all the rest. There is nothing more unorthodox than some views on fundamental matters expressed in the Haggadah. Thus e. g. the idea of a personal Messiah is rejected,[5] the last verses of Deuteronomy are ascribed to Joshua.[6] The Haggadah contains the statement that Job never lived.[7]

To substantiate my argument I shall cite the words of some great Jewish authorities. In his introduction to the Haggadah[8] Rabbi Abraham, son of the great Maimonides, and himself a great scholar, says,—"We are not obliged to defend the views of the sages of the Talmud concerning natural science, medicine or astrology, or concerning any other subject, simply on the ground that our sages were men of great knowledge in all matters and details touching the Torah.

"Whosoever propounds a certain theory or idea and expects it to be accepted on the mere ground of the author's eminence without substantiating its claims to truth and reasonableness, such a man acts against the Torah and contrary to human intelligence. The Lord said, 'Thou shalt not respect the poor, nor honor the great person. In righteousness shalt thou judge'.

"As far as the knowledge of the Torah is concerned,

---

[5] Babli Sanhedrin 98a.
[6] Babli Baba Batra 15a.
[7] Babli Baba Batra 15a. Cp. also Succah 5a.
[8] Maamar 'al odot Derashot Ḥazal, translated from Arabic into Hebrew by an unknown scholar, published in Kobes Teshubot ha-Rambam, ed. A. Lichtenstein, Leipzig 1859.

our sages have arrived at the highest possible perfection, but that is not the case as to any other branch of knowledge. The Rabbis themselves speak in that vein, when rejecting the medical theory propounded by a certain Rabbi, declaring that it proved untrue"(Talmud Babli Shabbat 66b).

In the course of his valuable essay Rabbi Abraham speaks of Derashot (haggadic explanations) which contain a figurative or hidden meaning, which are parabolical or hyperbolical expressions of some idea. Rabbi Abraham was mindful of the words of his illustrious father: "Beware that thou take not literally those sayings of our sages, for thou wouldst thereby degrade religion and find thyself in contradiction with the holy teaching. Always look for the deeper meaning and if thou art unable to find the kernel, leave the shell alone."

Rabbi Sherira Gaon, a very conservative talmudic authority of the tenth century, expresses himself very decidedly: "We do not consider Haggadah authoritative". See *Sefer Haeshkol*, II, 47ff.

Rabbi Samuel ha-Nagid[9] in his introduction to the Talmud says: "Haggadah—(that is any explanation in the Talmud on any subject outside the commandments)—you need not accept any of its teachings which do not appeal to your mind. You must know that of those laws which our sages have decided as Halakah, which are the traditions of Moses our teacher of blessed memory, nothing must be taken off, nor may anything be added to them. But when the sages indulge in explanations of biblical passages, each of them does according to what occurred to him and as it appeared good to his mind. Those explanations which appeal to us we accept, and the rest we do not consider authoritative."

[9] Samuel Halevi Ibn-Nagrela ha-Nagid, scholar, poet, statesman, 993–1055.

The late Dr. David Hoffmann, recognized as the greatest rabbinical authority of our age, who combined a comprehensive knowledge of the whole range of Jewish literature with modern scholarship, may be cited for his view (see Hoffmann, *Leviticus*, vol. 1, p. 6.). "The sayings of our sages called Haggadot contain a moral or an explanation of a scriptural passage not bearing upon Jewish law, or something similar. They are by no means to be considered divine traditions and we are not obliged to accept them." It is the more necessary to emphasize all this since Gentile scholars have been guilty of misstatements. See Dr. Perles' review of Bousset's *Religion des Judentums* (Berlin 1912). Schuerer's chapter on "Life under the Law," the above mentioned book by Bousset, and Weber's *Jewish Theology* have succeeded in creating an opinion about "Jewish Legalism" which is quite unjustified by the evidence of the original texts. Weber states: "Die midraschisch haggadischen Nationalwerke sind ebenso normative Lehrschriften als die halachischen."

Eisenmenger, his predecessors and successors, have preached a similar tale, and any story or parable or proverb of rabbinic lore, half understood or misinterpreted, was torn from its context and triumphantly displayed as a sample of the wickedness and folly of Jewish "doctrines". The "origin of the limping devil"[10] is one of the amusing instances of such unscholarly methods. The false light in which rabbinic lore has been placed has been shown up by Dr. Schechter in his *Aspects of Rabbinic Theology*, furthermore by Guedemann (*Das Judentum*, 1905), Wohlgemuth (*Das Jüdische Religionsgesetz*, 1913–14) and Gruenbaum (*Neue Beiträge* 1893.). It is very important to remember that there is no such thing as a systematic Jewish Theology. Even a system of fundamental points

---

[10] See Gruenbaum, *Gesammelte Aufsaetze* 2, p. 187.

of creed did not grow up before the times of the Karaites and then was evolved through the necessity of defending Judaism. Maimonides endeavored to condense Judaism into thirteen principles of faith, but, as Crescas rightly contends, they are both too many and too few.[10a] The Haggadah, while preaching the beauty of holy life, does not give us laws of belief and practice; the religious conduct of the Jew is regulated entirely by the Halakah. (But see S. Kaatz, *Die muendliche Lehre und ihr Dogma*, Leipzig 1922).

B. THE HAGGADAH OF THE CHRISTIAN FATHERS

Whereas in Jewish lore we had to differentiate between material referring to legal practices or principles of belief—Halakah—and Haggadah, devotional and ethical literature, the distinction to be made here is a more personal one. There is no definite line of demarcation between Haggadah and Dogma of the Christian Fathers; what is important is the personal standing of the Father in question. "The Fathers are spoken of according to their authority as greater or lesser" (Martin, *Catholic Religion*, p. 147). "Father" in itself does not imply absolute authority of anything he teaches, the word is used in the New Testament to mean a teacher of spiritual things by whose means the soul of man is born again into the likeness of Christ (*Catholic Encyclopaedia*, 6, p. 1). However, it naturally came about that the mass of traditions of the Church, handed down through generations of bishops and Fathers, acquired a certain amount of authority and "appeals to the Fathers are a subdivision of appeals to tradition. In the first half of the second century begin the appeals to the sub-apostolic age. Half a century later St. Irenaeus supplements this method by an appeal to the tradition handed down in every church by the succession of its bishops (Adv. Haer. III, 1–3), and Tertullian

[10a] See Responsa of R. Moses Sofer, Yoreh Deah, Pressburg 1841, No. 356, p. 153b.

clinches this argument by the observation that as all the churches agree, their tradition is secure, for they could not all have strayed by chance into the same error. The appeal is thus to the churches and their bishops, none but bishops being authoritative exponents of the doctrines of their churches" (*ibidem*).

In all matters of importance a consensus omnium was necessary. "It is an accepted principle that the *agreement of all the Fathers of the Church together* in matters of faith and morals, begets complete certainty and commands assent, because they, as a body, bear witness to the teachings and belief of the infallible Church. The consensus, however, need not be absolute; a moral agreement suffices; as e. g. when some of the *greatest* Fathers testify to a doctrine of the Church and the rest, though quite aware of it, do not oppose it. Whatever, therefore, the Fathers unanimously teach as the divinely revealed tradition of the Church must be accepted and believed as such." (Schmid, *Manual of Patrology*, cited above). A consensus of the Fathers is not of course expected in very small matters (*Cath. Enc.*, 6, p. 4).

It is obvious from the two quotations that no general law can be said to apply to the Haggadah of the Christian Fathers. In Jewish lore Haggadah is never authoritative. In Mohammedan lore it would be valid until the Isnād (see below) is found to be either forged or otherwise not in accordance with the rules laid down by the scholars of Hadith criticism. With the Haggadah of a Father of the Church it will be necessary to investigate the individual tradition for the following points: (1) Identity of the author, whether he is a greater or a lesser Father, (2) Importance of the theory or the story, i. e. is it weighty enough to require for its authentication the consensus omnium or at least of some of the greatest Fathers? (3) Has it been vouchsafed such

consent expressly or at least has it not been opposed?—
The difference between devotional and practical tradition
is hardly touched upon. The New Testament of course
is all authoritative. For non-Catholic views, see esp.
G. P. Fisher, *History of Christian Doctrine*, p. 41 f.[10b]

For the official declarations of the various denominations
see Schaff, *Creeds of Christendom*.

C. MOHAMMEDAN HAGGADAH

The Halakah of Jewish lore is represented in Moslem
literature by the Sunna and the traditional Hadith,
the Haggadah by the ethical and devotional Hadith.
Sunna is "der in der alten muhammedanischen Gemeinde
lebende Usus mit Bezug auf ein religiöses oder gesetz-
liches Moment." Hadith is the form in which the Sunna
was stated. Hadith originally meant "story", "report".
Later on it acquired the meaning of something reported
as a law, rite, sentiment, principle, which a companion
of the Prophet had witnessed or heard.

The Hadith consisted of two parts, the *silsul*, i. e. the
chain of authorities leading up to the Prophet or a companion of the Prophet; and the *matn*, the text of this
tradition. The chain of authorities, in its entirety called
Isnād, authenticates the Hadith. Now a Sunna may be
accompanied by such a Hadith, which would then lend

[10b] After I had written the above a letter reached me from Dr. H. P. Smith of
the Union Theological Seminary, who puts the matter very succinctly: "The Catholic
Religion recognizes as authoritative in doctrine not only the Scriptures of the Old and
New Testaments, but also the traditions which have always been received in the Church.
This includes the works of the Fathers, although when it comes to particular statements
of the Fathers questions arise easily and the actual practice is to use as a proof such as
agree with the great theologians, of which Thomas Aquinas is the chief. The reason
is that the Catholic believes the Church as an organism to have been divinely guided
so that its opinion is infallibly true. The Protestants, believing that the Catholic
authorities had corrupted the pure doctrine, rejected tradition and made the source
of doctrine the Scriptures, the Old Testament in Hebrew and the New Testament in
Greek. The reason is that Christ and his Apostles were held to be divinely guided so
that their statements must be received as true. This includes the Hebrew Scriptures,
because the New Testament writers recognized these as the word of God."

it additional strength, but the Sunna is in itself so strong that it remains valid even where no Hadith accompanies it.[11]

And whereas Sunna almost always deals with Laws and customs, there are also Hadiths of devotional and ethical content. And here we find an instructive parallel to the place Haggadah occupies in Jewish lore.

"We need not conclude," says Professor Goldziher,[12] "that there is not a grain of truth here and there in the Hadith communications of the later generations, coming, if not directly from the mouth of the Prophet, still from the oldest generation of Moslem authority. But on the other hand, one can easily perceive that the great distance from the source, both in respect to time and extent, brought with it the increasing danger of inventing doctrines whether of theoretical value or for practical purposes, in outwardly correct Hadith forms, and assigned to the Prophet and his companions as the highest authority."

This feature is the hallmark of Moslem tradition: no Jewish Rabbi or any Father of the Church employs it as thoroughly.[13] A special branch of science arose, the Hadith criticism, which aimed at separating the chaff from the wheat of genuine tradition.[14]

And with regard to this criticism the analogy referred to above is noteworthy. "The pia fraus of the inventors of tradition was met with forbearance on all sides, when

---

[11] For a very interesting parallel in Jewish law cp. Hoffmann, *Leviticus*, I, 4f., where the question is discussed as to whether Jewish Law, where its validity is not quite evident from the text, depends for this validity on the Midrashic interpretations of the verse in question, or whether these interpretations are not efforts at discovering a law, already valid, in the wording of the Pentateuchal text.

[12] Goldziher, *Muhammed und Islam*, 1917. I have also used his *Muham. Studien*, II, p. 1. ff.

[13] In the Talmud we find a string of two or three authorities, but that in itself would not assure the law any validity.—The Church Fathers also mention certain stories in the name of other older authorities.

[14] The comparison with Massorah almost forces itself upon one's consciousness, when dealing with Hadith criticism. The main difference seems to lie in the fact that the Massorah was in the main a preventive agency.

it was a question of *ethical* and *devotional* Hadith. Stricter theologians, however, assumed a more serious attitude when ritualistic practices or legal judgments were to be founded on such Hadith" (Goldziher, *ibid.*, p. 50)

Chapter I

THE NATURE OF ANGELS

(A) In Jewish Literature

1. *Biblical.* The angels are the messengers of God executing His will. As such they bring man both reward and punishment, even as they act in accordance with God's command. They visit the tent of Abraham[15] and bring him good tidings, while to Lot they convey an evil message. An angel warns Balaam, coming upon him as an "adversary", addresses Gideon, etc. In the heavens they sing God's graces, they are His host. In the pre-exilic books of the Hebrew Bible there appears no name of any angel. Clearly, "The names of the angels came from Babylon" (*Gen. Rabbah* 18.2)

2. *Post-biblical*: Rabbinic lore has more to say about them. But it does not either add or take away any of those attributes with which any reader of the Hebrew Bible finds them endowed. In rabbinic literature, the angels are essentially God's dutiful servants. They do His will and sing His praise. They take part in His counsels, and though holy, are capable of error, but not of transgression. The spirit of truth and the spirit of Justice oppose the creation of man, fearing he might do only wrong. They are amazed at Adam's bright splendor and would have worshipped him, were it not for the Almighty who showed them, by letting him fall into a deep sleep, that Adam was only mortal. They err when talking

---

[15] See Gen. R. *ad. loc.*

innocently of Sodom's impending ruin, but they are good by nature. No law would be too heavy a burden for them. It would overtax Israel, and therefore the sages insist: "The Torah was not given to the ministering angels".[16] Again and again this sentence occurs, intimating that no law would be too hard for angels, who are not tempted by evil.[17]

The Angels have no Yeṣer Hara' (Evil inclination), they have only one heart; man has two hearts, the good and the evil Yeṣer. Only the generation of Deborah was angelic in this respect. Angels are created every day, who sing praise to the Lord and vanish into the stream of fire whence they came. They have justified their existence by praising God, which is their raison d'être (Ḥagigah 12 f.).

A Midrash cited in Ṣemaḳ (*Sepher Miṣwot Ḳatan* by Isaac of Corbeil, 1280) reads: "When God created the world, He produced on the second day the angels with their natural inclination to do good and an absolute incapacity for sin." "Angels have no evil will and are thus spared jealousy, covetousness, lust and other passions." "There is neither ill-will, nor discord among them" (Shabb. 89a; Gen. R. 48. 11; Sifre, Numb., 42).[18]

Yer. Berakot 9a: Rabbi Simeon b. Joḥai, commenting on Deut. 28, 10: "And *all* the people of the earth shall see that Thou art called by the name of the Lord, and they shall fear Thee"—says: "all" includes spirits and demons, all of whom recognize the dignity of Israel keeping God's commandments.

---

[16] Babli Berakot 25b; Me'ilah 14b.

[17] In Deut. Rabba XI Moses is said to refer to a battle in heaven. In answer to Samael's call to give up his soul he says:..."At the age of eighty I took part in the battle of the angels..and I triumphed in the circle on high (the divine host) and revealed their secret to man." The whole chapter is full of late interpolations. See M. Rosenfeld, *Der Midrash Deuteronomium Rabba*, Berlin 1899, p. 79. The sources of Deut. Rabbah are late. See Zunz, *Gottesdienstliche Vorträge* 2te Auflage, p. 264.

[18] For the goodness and benevolence of the angels see further: Pesiḳta Rab. II, Yelammedenu on Numbers XII, Midr. Shem Tob on Ps. 17.7. For their purity and holiness see Pesiḳta 108b, Tanḥ. Exodus XXIII, Pes. Rab. 16.

Kiddushin 40b (Text Job 25.2. "Dominion and awe are His: He maketh peace in His high places."): "If God had to make peace among the angels who are ruled neither by jealousy, hatred, discord, strife or party quarrels, how much more necessary is it to make peace among men who are subject to all those passions!"

Canticles 8.13: "The companions hearken to Thy voice because it is sweet. "M. Rabba *ad loc.*" The companions are the angels; they are so called because neither enmity, nor jealousy, hatred, discord, strife or schism prevails among them."

In the description of the seven heavens, both in Abot de R. Nathan and in the Pesikta Rabbeti, where all possible details about angels are given, there is no reference to fallen angels. These books are comparatively uninfluenced by foreign lore. Whilst the "serpent" (Gen. 3.1 ff.) is very suggestive and thus allows a large amount of legends to cluster round the chapter, the angels are conceived as beyond sins or falls.

A very valuable support for this view is contained in the following legend of the Babylonian Talmud. (Shabbat 88b).

"When Moses ascended to heaven, the ministering angels said unto the Holy One blessed be He: 'Sovereign of the Universe, what has one born of a woman to do among us?' He answered: 'He is come to receive the Torah'. 'What!' said they unto Him, 'art Thou to bestow upon mere flesh and blood that treasured gem which has been with Thee for 974 generations before the world was created?' The Holy One blessed be He then bade Moses answer the Angels. Moses said: 'Is it not written in your Torah, Thou shalt have no other gods before Me? Do you (the Angels) live amongst idolaters (that this prohibition could apply to you)?...Again, is it not written therein, Thou shalt not murder, thou shalt not commit adultery, thou shalt not steal? Does jealousy, does an evil inclination exist among you?..'.".

The question is a rhetorical one, the answer being clearly: Since these interdictions refer only to fallible men and cannot refer to impeccable angels, the angels were wrong in asking, "Confer Thy glory upon the heavens", meaning, "Keep Thy Torah among us". Now, convinced of their error, they say: "O Lord, how excellent is Thy Name on all the earth!" but they do not repeat the second sentence, "Confer Thy glory upon the heavens", for the Torah is clearly meant for the earth.[19] (Psalm 8.10).

[19] The author is, of course, but too well aware of the fact that folk-lore accounts must not be taken literally and that stories are bound to be mixed, so that characteristics and details and embellishments freely interchange. Also "fama crescitur eundo", each teller of a tale adding some ingenious detail. Nevertheless I cannot forbear appending a note on the relation subsisting between the "Creation of the Angels and their fall".

Numbers 11. According to Yalḳuṭ Ḥadash, the angels were created before the world, emanating from God's glorious Light. Dan. 7.10 and Hagigah 14b are too visionary even for the Haggadah to be considered in this connection. Genesis 1.26 and Job 38.7 seem to agree that angels were created before the world. In the former place God says: "Let us make", which, though it has been explained as pluralis maiestatis, seems more naturally to refer to His host whom he informs of His intention. Philo *ad loc.* refers to the divine beings who surround the throne of God, as written in Job 1.6; Dan. 4.14. The Haggadah has seized upon this as a fertile ground to work on.

Hitzig (*Isaiah*, p. 65) compares our verse with Genesis 11.7 where נרדה (plural) obviously has cohortative meaning. He thus repeats the opinion of R. Ami who (Gen. Rabba VIII) says "God took counsel with His own heart".

From Job 38.7, "When the morning stars sang together and all the sons of God shouted for joy", it is still clearer that the angels were present at the creation of the earth, though this passage might easily be made to agree with the conception that the angels were created on the first day.

The Book of Jubilees, 3, tells of some angels created on the first day. According to Genesis Rabba 1.3 the angels were not created before the second day lest people think they had assisted God in His creative work (See also P. d. R. E. IV). Rabbi Ḥaninah (*ibidem*) identifies the angels with the "fowl that flies upon the earth, upon the face of the expanse of the heavens", supporting his theory from Isaiah 11.2. (According to this interpretation the angels were created on the fifth day; some of them object to the creation of man on the sixth day and are burned).

Tabari I.83. On the authority of Ibn Anas: God created the angels on the 4th day and the Jinn on the 5th day and Adam on Friday. And some of the Jinn became infidels. The Cave of Treasure (*Schatzhöhle* ed. Bezold) gives a more detailed account:

Creation of Angels	first day	(cp. Jubilees)
Creation of Man	sixth day	first hour
Fall of Satan	sixth day	second hour
Adam enters Paradise	sixth day	third hour
Fall of Man	sixth day	ninth hour

Thus Adam lived in Paradise but six hours. Rabbi Akiba too holds this view but both are refuted. Rabbi Johanan (Other versions have: Aḥa, Ḥama Bar Ḥanina of the 2nd

We have thus, for the incapacity of angels to sin, both the very eloquent argumentum e silentio of Abot de R. Nathan and the Pesikta Rabbeti, as well as the positive statements quoted above (Gen. Rabba 48.11). "The Yeṣer Hara‘ has no power over angels" (cp. Babli Sanhedrin 38b).

All this makes it quite clear that it would have appeared blasphemous to the Jewish mind to have angels cast down from Heaven for transgressing in any coarse manner. Even Mohammed and his followers take this view. (See Koran, Sura II, 28–32, which is obviously borrowed from Jewish sources. The angels admit: "Praise be unto Thee, we have no knowledge but what Thou teachest us, for Thou art knowing and wise").

We find, however, that some angels because of their loquacity are reduced to a lower state. All this bears out the fundamental point that the main theme of fallen angels is un-Jewish. Furthermore, side by side with the interpretation of Bible passages misused for angelological purposes, there runs both in Christian and Mohammedan literature

and 3rd generations of Amoraim [3rd century and beginning of 4th]) bar Ḥaninah said (In Abot de Rabbi Nathan it is related anonymously. See also Pes. R. ed. Friedman, p. 187b.): "That day (the sixth day of the Creation) has twelve hours. In the first his (Adam's) dust was heaped up; in the second he became a shapeless mass; in the third his limbs were shaped (stretched); in the fourth the soul was put (lit. sprinkled) into him; in the fifth he stood upon his feet; in the sixth he called (the beasts by their) names; and in the seventh Eve was joined to him; in the eighth the two united and became four (Cain and Abel); in the ninth he was forbidden to eat of the tree; in the tenth he did wrong; in the eleventh he was sentenced; in the twelfth he was driven out, and departed."

Thus נעשה in Gen. 26 is pluralis maiestatis, or the Haggadists would explain it by means of the principle of אין מוקדם ומאוחר בתורה. "The historical narratives in the Torah are not necessarily arranged in systematic order." (Babli Pesaḥim 6b). The angels who were burned because of their objection to the creation of man lived then but three or four days, unless they were created before. Lucifer too must have revolted before the sixth day or all "Ersatztheorien" fall to the ground.

Lucifer fell thus:
(1) Before the creation.
(2) As Satan after the creation, having seduced Adam and Eve.
(3) Leading his troop to the daughters of man.

He did not fall for objecting to the creation of man, either because he had fallen before, or because he had sworn revenge on man and thus would wish him created, or because his advice was not asked.

the natural exegesis. Judaic teaching from Rabbi Simon bar Yoḥai down to Hillel ben Samuel (13th century)[20] protests against the former, and even the Samaritans take the natural sense of the passages in the Bible.

Disputed Passages

The Septuagint on Job is held to convey definite teaching of fallen angels. Seeing that the translators of the Hebrew Scriptures into Greek were of diverse kinds, exact translators and adherents of definite theses to which the text was subjected, this view may not be considered to be wrong. But the passages in question do not bear the meaning imputed to them.

33.23. "If a thousand death-dealing angels should be (against him) not one of them shall wound him."

36.14. "May their soul perish in their youth, may their life be wounded by the angels!"

21.15. "The riches unjustly accumulated shall be vomited up, angels shall drag him out of his house."

In all these passages there is not the slightest evidence in favor of the assumption that the angels are acting in the interest of evil, and not rather as servants of God.

Philo, *De Gigantibus* VII f. A spiritualized version of the story connected with Genesis 6.1–4. Some of the souls who were part of the universal soul "somehow stooped from their pure dwelling in the air to incarnation in human bodies, leaving behind them an incorruptible group of fellow-souls, whom God used as His ministers for the supervision of mortals, and whom Moses called angels. Of these incarnate souls, some were able to resist the current of sensuous life and to return to their original abode, the

---

[20] Hillel Ben Samuel, cited by Epstein in "Eldad had-Dani" ch. 9. He objected in strenuous words to that interpretation. See also Eliezer Ashkenasi, Ta'am Zekenim 70ff., Edelman, Ḥemdah Genuzah 18ff, and Guedemann, Geschichte 2, 170f.

others, surrendering themselves to restless activities, were engulfed in the illusory world of wealth, fame and similar unreal things".

See Prof. Kennedy's summary, who compares Plato's "young gods", to whom souls (who had previously formed part of the universal soul in mortal bodies) were entrusted.

Philo's angels are the angels of the Hebrew Bible. Cp. *De Opificio Mundi, passim.*

Fallen Angels in Job 4.18.

"Lo, in His servants He puts no trust and His angels (or Messengers) He chargeth with folly."

This is often regarded as a definite statement of the Fall of Angels. Now we are ready to admit that the next verse with its emphasis on

> "How much more them that dwell in houses of clay.
> Whose foundation is in the dust.
> Who are crushed before the moth!"

clearly implies that "His messengers" are not earthly beings. And in face of this the Targum, "Lo, in His servants the prophets He trusteth not and in His ambassadors He findeth folly" will not be considered sufficient evidence to the contrary; and the fact that rabbinic literature, though offering several comments, appears to take the sentence in the light of the Targum, will only prove that the Jews at any rate found "Prophets"="Men of God" quite a good contrast to the ordinary mortal.

However that may be, another point not to be forgotten is that the sentence, though apparently referring to angels, does not by any means imply a "fall". That angels were imperfect in knowledge is evident in the Bible itself. Satan is an angel of God whose office it is to tempt man and to accuse him. Yet he indulges in vain hopes as to his capacity of causing Job to sin with his lips. And he finds himself rebuked on another occasion, when accusing "the brand plucked out of the fire" (Zech. 3.2). The sentence may also express the consciousness of an essential difference between God and the angels, the Lord and His servants. They may be foolish, but that does not imply rebellion. Open disobedience on the part of the angels to the Law of God is foreign to the Hebrew Scriptures. Not even Satan rebels; he errs and is rebuked.

(B) IN CHRISTIAN LITERATURE

Angels in N. T. The conception of their functions is to a great degree dependent on Septuagint passages. They suffer a degradation and an elevation in comparison with the angelology of the Hebrew Bible. They are degraded in that they can sin, fall, even rebel; they are elevated in that they take the place of God. Acts 7.30, 38; cp. Heb. 2.2. An angel spoke to Moses and to "our fathers" on Mount Sinai; he received and transmitted the oracles.[21]

They become much more familiar entities than they are in the Hebrew Bible. We hear details about their life. They accompany Jesus through his earthly life, they will prepare the day of Judgment, they see his resurrection.

The Jewish tradition about angels lingers on; it is frequent in Gregory I, e. g. *Moralia* 18.71; 27.66; 2.38.

Augustine *on Angels. Enchiridion* XIV. "For it is possible that a man or *an angel* may not be unjust. But except a man or an angel there cannot be any one that is unjust."

Ibid. XV. "Nor was there absolutely any source whence originally evil should arise except from the good nature of angel and man."[22]

---

[21] For parallels in Babylonian lore of the New Testament conception of two Empires see Sayce, Gifford Lectures, 1901 p. 315 ff. 361f. There two "sons of a deity" are angels.

[22] Augustine explains in the preceding passage that by "good nature" he means "will".

XXVII. "The mass of the whole human race under condemnation was lying in evil...and joined to the side of those angels who had sinned, was paying the deserved penalty of impious apostacy." "There is no renewing (*reformatio*) for impious angels."

ibid. "Certain angels through impious pride deserting God were cast down from their high heavenly habitation into the lowest darkness of this air." Some of them are infallible, like the angels of Jewish lore (*ibid.*).

Of Continence VI. "God chose to make man such that at first it might be a good desert to him not to sin, and after a just reward not to be able to sin. For such also at the last will He make His Saints, as to be without all power to sin. Such forsooth even now hath He His Angels, whom in Him we so love, as to have no fear for any of them, lest by sinning he become a devil." (For this curious differentiation we have, in our discussion of Gregory's statements, endeavored to account). See the remarks on the homily of Aelfric, where the genesis of this theory is given.

The Nature of Angels. Gregory V. 38. Text: Job 4.18.
"Behold in His servants He put no trust.
And in His angels He found folly."

"Though the angelical nature, by being fixed in the contemplation of the Creator, remains unchangeable in its own state, yet hereby, that it is a created being, it admits in itself the variableness of change. Now to be changed is to go from one thing into another, and to be without stability in one's self. For every single being tends to some other thing by steps, as many in number as it is subject to motions of change. And it is only the incomprehensible Nature which knows not to be moved from its fixed state, in that it knows not to be changed from this, that it is always the same. For if the essence of the angels had been strange to the notion of change, being created well by its Maker, it would never have fallen in the case of reprobate spirits from the tower of its blessed estate. But Almighty God in a marvellous manner framed the nature of the highest spiritual existences good, yet at the same time capable of change: that both, they that refused to remain, might meet with ruin, and they that continued in their own state of creation, might henceforth be established therein more worthily in proportion as it was owing to their own choice, and become so much the more meritorious in God's sight, as they had stayed the motion of their mutability by the establishing of the will. Whereas then this very angelical nature too is in itself mutable, which same mutability it has hereby overcome, in that it is bound by the chains of love for Him, who is ever the same, it is now rightly said 'Behold His servants are not steadfast'.

"And there is forthwith added a proof of this same mutability, in that it is brought in from the case of the apostate spirits, 'And in His angels He found folly'. And from the fall of these He rightly draws the consideration of human frailty."

LXX. (The proper translation is: "Behold He putteth no trust in His servants"). The Vulgate has: "Ille ne suis quidem servis credit et angelos suos temeritatis insimulat". It appears therefore that our instance is one of the many which may be called haggadistic translations ad hoc. The whole force of Gregory's argument, as made to fit our sentence, depends upon this paraphrase. I have appended this extract of Gregory's commentary, because it gives a fair picture of the mental difficulties which he found facing him. There were two currents of views concerning angels. The first, in accordance with all the references to them in the Hebrew Bible, flourished in Jewish tradition. The angels, created as servants of God, have no free will, being only good, and nothing else. On the other hand, Gregory heard as authentic stories of fallen angels. He had to reconcile these conflicting reports. For, whereas in later Jewish literature, the view that angels *can* sin, was always felt to be haggadistic in so far as it did not at any time loom in the creed, tradition or rites of later Judaism, the Christian Fathers do not give the impression of having discriminated as to their importance between these and stories of the Hebrew Bible. Jerome may be said to form one of the few exceptions. However that may be, Gregory finds himself on the horns of a dilemma and, unconsciously, argues in a vicious circle, basing his statements now on the text, now on the traditions.

Gregory, *Moralia* II, 20. Text. I Kings 22, 19ff. "The right hand of God is the elect portion of the angels and the left hand of God signifies the *reprobate portion* of Angels. For not alone do the good serve God by the aid which they render, but *likewise the wicked* by the trials which they inflict; not only they who lift upward them that are turning from transgression but they who press down those who refuse to turn back. Nor, because it is called the host of heaven, are we hindered from understanding therein the reprobate portion of the angels, for whatsoever birds we know to be poised in the air we call them the birds of heaven." This is the tone of genuine Midrash. It seems to represent unalloyed "Jewish Angelology", except for the adjectives "wicked" and "reprobate". Jewish lore knows no such beings standing at the left hand of God or identified with Him. מלאכי חבלה (destroying angels) is what the Jewish texts would read. Even the מזיקין (evil spirits) accept God's dominion. The מלאכי חבלה are just as good as the angels sent to bless man. Their natures are identical; they are messengers and servants of the Almighty.

Gregory, *Moralia* II, 3. "Who are called the sons of God, saving the elect angels?[23] They never so go forth from the vision of God, as to be deprived of the joys of interior contemplation. For, if when they went forth, they lost the vision of the Creator, they could neither have raised up the fallen, nor announced the truth to those in ignorance."[24]

(C) In Mohammedan Literature

Kazvini (*ed. Wuestenfeld, I, 12*) on the Nature of Angels. "Know thou that the angels are substances (beings) free from the darkness of passion and the turbidity of wrath, never rebelling against the commandments of God, but always doing what they are commanded to do.

"Their food is the praise of God, and their drink the description of His holy and pure being...

"There is not a span of space in the heavens upon which no angel is to be found prostrating himself in prayer."

Chapter 2

THE TWO SATANS

(A) Bible

There is an essential difference between the serpent of the third chapter of Genesis and the Satan of the New Testament (Roskoff, *Geschichte des Teufels*, p. 191). According to the Zendavesta, Angromainyus, pregnant with death, leaps from heaven in the form of a serpent, a form

---

[23] What about Genesis 6.4? The answer would either be that Gregory follows his teacher Augustine in not identifying "Bene Elohim" of that passage with angels, or that he would explain it by having reference to the points outlined on the preceding page.

[24] The theory being that the angels who sinned and fell had gone forth, lost the vision of the Creator and thus their angelic nature.

in which he appears regularly or at least often. In Genesis as in the Avesta, the ancestors of the human tribe are destined to happiness, so long as they live in harmony with their Creator. According to Zoroastrian speculation, darkness has become evil because it envied light; Meshia and Meshiana, who had been created by Ahura Mazda as pure beings, are drawn to Angromainyus through envy. Thus the fallen angel of Luther agrees with Angromainyus but not with the serpent of Genesis. According to the Persian myth Angromainyus sets himself as an *independent power* against Ahura Mazda and when thus "das Uebel und nach späterer Entwicklung das Böse wirklich vorhanden ist," the war between the powers becomes possible. Man, a creation of Ahura Mazda, becomes the object of the contest and so must oppose Angromainyus. According to the Jewish conception, Man, in sinning, follows his own will, thus acting against the divine will. According to Genesis, the source of evil is in man himself who should not have eaten of the forbidden fruit. In Vendidad the serpent is the evil principle itself and the cause of man's sin is envy. Genesis knows nothing of that, only in the Book of Wisdom (2.24) is this theory to be found. If this book be free from Christian interpolation—and that is a moot point,— the above theory may be the result of a Jew's acquaintance with Persian lore, easily accessible in exile. Alexandrian Judaism, of which the Book of Wisdom is a fruit, had appropriated Hellenistic and Zoroastrian speculation. Thus the serpent of Genesis became the representative (tool) of evil.

Satan in the Hebrew Bible

Among the angels of God there is one called Satan. His task is to accuse man, to doubt his piety (Job. 1.6), to put all obstacles in his way that he may fall and sin.

He would of course charge man the more for a crime really committed (Zech.3.1). He is even permitted to afflict him that man's firmness of belief may be established (Job 1.6). But stress must be laid on the word "permitted". Job suffers because God (Job 1.12; 2.6) expressly consents to the trials he has to undergo. Satan never appears as acting on his own account; he acts in his capacity as God-appointed accuser and tempter (Job. 13.ff; Zech 3. 1; 1 Ch. 21.1). When he accuses without reason he is rebuked (Zech. 3.1) and silenced.

Never and in no place do we hear of any act or utterance that might imply disobedience to God or rebellious intentions against His authority. Being one of God's servants he is a necessary part of the heavenly hierarchy, by reason of his office of importance in the life of man. How fully Satan is conceived and described as but a tool of God, may be inferred from the fact that God Himself is represented as tempting man.[25] Satan, then, as God's appointed tempter, acts on His behalf, at His command.

As in Job, so in other places he is represented as a messenger of God. He has no private reasons for tempting man, nor special joy in causing his fall. God desires man to be perfect and Satan accuses and tests man in order that his sincerity may be proved or his fickleness punished.

God is One, none dares challenge His authority, that is the red thread running through the Hebrew Bible.[26]

---

[25] Cp. I Sam, 26.19; I Chron. 21.1.

[26] *Schrader on the two Satans.* (Schrader, *Die Keilinschriften und das Alte Testament, 3te Auflage*, p. 463ff). "Anderer (als der alttestamentliche Satan) obwohl wahrscheinlich im letzten Grunde ebenfalls babylonischer Herkunft, ist dagegen die erst später auftretende und namentlich im Neuen Testament ausgedehnt vorliegende Vorstellung von Satan als dem obersten Fürsten des widergöttlichen Geisterreiches. Dieser Zug in der Gestalt des Teufels, der in späterer Zeit fast ausschliesslich in den Vordergrund tritt, geht vielmehr mit der grössten Wahrscheinlichkeit, wenn auch wieder vermittelt durch eine persische Zwischenstufe, im letzten Grunde auf die Gestalt des Gegners des Lichtgottes im babylonischen Drachenkampfe und auf die diesem Kampfe vorausgegangene Spaltung in der Götterwelt zurück." For the way by which the New Testament Satan came from Persia see Bousset, *Göttinger Gelehrte Anzeigen*, 1905.

Passages in the Hebrew Bible Referring to Satan or Demons

(1) Deuteronomy 32.17 refers to heathen gods (or demons, the Satyrs) to whom the Jews were offering sacrifices.

(2) 1 Chron. 21.1 speaks of Satan as provoking David to sin; in 2 Sam. 24.1 God is said to have done so. This may be due to the author's desire not to let God appear as seducer, or to emphasize the fact that it is Satan's office to tempt. Probably a combination of both was at work.

(3) Zech. 3.1. Lange, *Genesis* p. 90, is surely wrong in speaking of "Bezeichnung des Satans als Gottesfeindes, als des von Gott abgefallenen Stifters einer bösen Reichsmacht gegenüber der Gründung eines Reiches Gottes".

"And he showed me Joshua the High Priest standing before the angel of the Lord and Satan standing at his right hand to be adversary. And the Lord said unto Satan 'The Lord rebuke thee, Satan, yea, the Lord that has chosen Jerusalem rebuke thee. Is not this a brand plucked out of the fire?'" And Satan vanishes. He has accused without reason and reaps reproach. There is no trace of disobedience; the angel, like himself a minister of God, defeats him. There is no opposition to God. Satan opposes Israel, for it is his office to go to and fro and find fault with man and especially so with the chosen people. There is no fight for man, as between Ahriman and Ormuzd. Satan accuses, desiring naked justice, God is merciful and Satan has to retire rebuked. As in Job there is no joy in his attack, nor any display of sadness at the failure of his efforts. Satan is not the evil principle, but an instrument for good. He stands alone in his attack, the only accuser, no band with him, no trace of a rival dominion or of an empire beside, and hostile to, God's.

(4) Job 1 and 2 are so clearly against any Satan vs. God theory that it will be sufficient if just the salient points

are noted. Satan appears among the sons of God, not as an opponent of His will, for he would otherwise not have been permitted to appear amongst the angels. He doubts Job's sincerity as a routine of his Satanic office. He has no joy in evil.

(5) Isaiah 27.1. "In that day the Lord with His sore and great and strong sword shall punish Leviathan the gliding serpent and Leviathan the crooked serpent, and He shall slay the dragon that is in the sea." 'The dragon that is in the sea' is undoubtedly Egypt. Cp. Isaiah 51.9 and Ezekiel 32.2. In verse 12 are named the country of the Euphrates and Assur besides Egypt. This makes it quite clear that the two Leviathans are Assur with Nineveh on the Tigris and Chaldea with Babel on the Euphrates. Nineveh on the Tigris, "auf dessen raschen Lauf und furchtbare Stromschnellen sein hebraisierter Name Ḥidekel hindeutet. Deshalb wird Assur einer flüchtigen, eilfertigen, gestreckten Laufes sich bewegenden Schlange verglichen, Babel dagegen einer gewundenen d. i. in schlangenlinichten Krümmungen sich windenden, weil es am vielgewundenen und gerade bei Babel labyrinthisch gewundenen Euphrat lag." (Franz Delitzsch, *Isaiah*, fourth edition, page 305). These texts, as has been shown, bear no evidence of any developments of the Satan of Genesis in the direction of his representation in the N. T.

Isaiah 14.12–16: *The "Lucifer" Legend.*

There is one passage in Isaiah, which for many centuries had been suffered to remain misinterpreted.

> "How art thou fallen from heaven,
> O day-star, son of the morning!
> How art thou cut down to the ground,
> Which didst lay prostrate the nations,
> And thou saidst in thy heart,

'I will ascend into heaven,
Above the stars of God,
Will I exalt my throne, etc. etc.;'
They that saw thee do narrowly look upon thee,
They gaze earnestly at thee!
Is this the man that made the earth to tremble,
That did shake kingdoms?"

It requires but a careful reading of the text to see that the chapter as a whole, and each verse individually, can refer only to the King of Babel; vv. 17, 13, and 19 are especially absurd if taken to refer to an angel. (Equal violence has been done to Ps. 82.7).

Luther was one of the first Christians to reject that interpretation. And it is interesting to note how much was built on it. Satan and his rebellious ranks owe their existence to a mistake, not of any Creator, but of the commentator of a prophetic passage. One of the latest authorities to doubt whether the conception of Satan's fall originated in Jewish lore or if it was read into it afterwards, is E. Schrader. Professor Driver (in *The Ideals of the Prophets*) is another modern scholar who has emancipated himself from the traditional misinterpretation of our passage, on which all the legends about rebellious angels are built. (See also J. Bewer, *The Literature of the O. T.*) They are thus un-Jewish in origin, and due to dualistic influences, to which, superficially, the language of 14.12 lent itself.

(B) Talmud

In the following places it is assumed that our chapter refers to the king of Babylon. *Babli Shabbat* 149 b: Rabbi Joḥanan said: "During the whole lifetime of that wicked man no creature laughed, for it is said:

'All the earth is at rest, is quiet;
They break forth into singing.'
From this it follows that till now there was no joyful cry."
He comes down to Sheol, as any other wicked man (*ibidem*).[27] Rabbi Joḥanan said: "What answer gave the Bath Kol[28] to the wicked one when he said, 'I will ascend into heaven above the heights of the clouds; I will be like the most High?' The Bath Kol came forth and said: 'Thou wicked man, son of a wicked man and descendant of the wicked Nimrod who caused, during his reign, all the world to revolt against Me! How many are the years of man? Seventy years or, even by reason of strength, fourscore years. Now from earth to heaven one must journey five hundred years, the thickness of the heavens is equal to a journey of 500 years, and between the lowest heaven and the next there is another journey of 500 years, and between each heaven and heaven...But to Sheol shalt thou be brought down, to the recesses of the pit.'"

(C) MIDRASH

Exodus Rabba 15.7. "Nebuchadnezzar worshipped the sun, for it is said: 'How art thou fallen from heaven, O shining one, son of the dawn!'" That is a very curious interpretation. It means apparently that when Nebuchadnezzar fell, the sun, his god, was proved powerless and thus 'fell from heaven.' (See Hirsch, in *JQR, New Series* vol. XIII, 1922).

Leviticus Rabba 18.7 explains the passage as referring to Nebuchadnezzar. See also Targum Sheni on Esther I and Exodus Rabba 8.2, which combines Isaiah 14 with Daniel 4. (Nebuchadnezzar had deified himself and therefore God degraded him to the state of an animal).

---

[27] In Ḥagigah more details are given. In Ḥullin 89a it is expressly stated that our passage refers to Nebuchadnezzar, hence Rashi's statement Shabb. 149b.

[28] 'Daughter of Voice'—heavenly voice. See Bacher, *Terminologie* II, 207.

Pirke de Rabbi Eliezer, ch. 35: "And he showed him the prince of the kingdom of Babylon ascending seventy rungs and descending. And he showed him the prince of the kingdom of Rome ascending, and he was not descending, but was saying 'I will be like the most High'. Jacob replied to him, 'Yet shalt thou be brought down to Sheol, to the uttermost part of the pit'. The Holy One, blessed be He, said to him, 'Even though thou shouldst make thy nest as high as the eagle' (Isaiah 14.14 combined with Jeremiah 19.16)."

Numbers Rabba 9.30: "Nebuchadnezzar made himself a little cloud and dwelt therein, as it is said, 'I shall ascend, etc.' God said: 'Thou saidst, I shall ascend, but I will bring thee low!' And he changed him into a beast."

Ruth Rabba 33. "The wicked being referred to was human." He has not repented while in this world and therefore he has no hope in the next.

Midrash Tehillim Ps. 82.7 combines that sentence with Isaiah 24.21. See also P.d.R.E., 47.

(D) Apocrypha

The book of Enoch has a great deal of non-Jewish lore, much of it to be found again in the N. T. Satan is the lord of the kingdom of evil. It is hard to say whether the Watchers continue the Satan tradition (13.5; 14.5; 64.4, 6). Though they tempt and accuse man and punish the condemned, they themselves also sin; whilst Satan, though he may be overzealous in the performance of his duties, never sins.

Book of Wisdom[29] 2.13: "He nameth himself a child of God." 2.16: "And he vaunteth that God is his father." The chapter is otherwise reminiscent of Isaiah 53, John 5.24,

---

[29] The author was an Alexandrian, of a time before Philo and after Jesus Sirach He was influenced by Greek philosophy. See Schürer, III, p. 357 f.

and I Corinth. 15.26. See also Freudenthal, *Die Flavius Josephus zugeschr. Schrift.*

Judaism has had an influx of demons from Persia of which Lilith, the Shedim, etc. are representatives (see *KAT.*, third edit.). But they do not influence Judaism, its theology or any fundamental belief. The name Satan does not imply enmity to God. The angel who opposes Balaam, does so because Balaam had provoked the anger of the Lord. He comes as a God-appointed opposer, Numb. 22.22. But Christianity accepts the Persian view of a rival God fully, and in one place especially, John 35.1, it is said: "To this end was the son of God manifested that he might destroy the works of the devil."[30]

(E) SATAN IN THE NEW TESTAMENT

Here he plays an entirely different rôle. First of all he is, next to God and Jesus, the predominant figure. He is independent, prince of the world (John 12.31), he challenges God, tempts Jesus (Matth. 4). God must fight him (Rom. 16.20), He throws him from heaven, casts him into an abyss (Rev. 12.9, 23); but God's power is not unlimited, for after 1000 years Satan will come up again and the fight will ensue afresh. He is a power of his own. Two camps, two empires and two kings are in the supernatural world, mutually exclusive. They fight one another. The devil is strong and Jesus must try his hardest to defeat him. He is represented as God's enemy from the beginning (John 8.44). He acts as God's enemy by betraying man. All crimes are attributed to his direct or indirect influence. He has ministers of his own (Matth. 35.41) who serve him in the pursuit of his man-hating designs (Rev. 12.7). Whilst on earth he seduces Eve (Rev. 12.13, 15) and leads her posterity astray.

[30] Cp. 1 John 5.19 with Deut. Rabba 11, where Samael comes to bring the soul of Moses to God. See also Baba Batra 16a.

He enters into men or women and causes them to be mad (Matth. 12.22); his servants enter into them. God or Jesus drives them out (*ibid*). It is a prominent part of Jesus' vocation to fight Satan's influence. In detail, by driving the devils out of the body of the possessed; in principle, by crushing in the end, Satan's empire. For, in spite of his fall, Satan is in the heavens and in fulness of time is to be driven thence (cp. Rev. 12.7; 16.4; 20.7). He exists thus, in heaven itself, the representative of an empire opposed to God, in full agreement with the conception of the two warring powers in the Avesta and in complete contradiction to the Satan of the Hebrew Bible.

I have discussed every verse of interest on this view in the Hebrew Scriptures. It has been said that the N. T. merely took over a Satan whom Judaism had already. All of the above verses contradict this statement. Besides, if that were the case, Jewish tradition would have shown some trace of a Satan as described in the N. T. The Mishna gives us the point of view of Jew and Judaism from very early times till 200 C. E., but there is not the slightest indication of such beliefs or views. Even Azazel, who to many seems to suggest demonology, is there conceived as the mountain whence the scapegoat was hurled down. Positive evidence of belief in demons and the power of driving them out—besides this argumentum ex silentio—is to be found in the fact that Rabbi Ishmael forbade his nephew to be miraculously healed by Jacob of Shekonya, a disciple of Jesus (Abodah Zarah 27b, and also Numbers Rabba 19).

To sum up: The Satan of the Hebrew Bible is part and parcel of monotheism; there is but one power, God. The Satan of the New Testament is a product of several sources. Babylonian and Greek mythology are laid under obligation. These factors did not work on the writers of the Hebrew

Scriptures. Greek and Persian lore began to play on the Jewish mind only after the greatest part of the Hebrew Bible was written. They come in for their share in the Apocrypha, are repelled by the Haggadah, which they enter in very small rivulets, appearing in late sources. But they play fully on the authors of the N.T. They are an indispensable element of the new structure. Jesus, crucifixion, eschatology, to mention three of the main problems, are absolutely dependent on the N. T. conception of Satan. The great influence of the monotheistic principle in Judaism may be inferred from the fact that no Haggadah, no Midrash, contains any hint of an empire independent of, and opposed to, God.

The Story of Lucifer. (As fully developed in Aelfric). Among the angels God had created was one excellent in beauty and great in office. He fell in love with himself and aspired to take the place of his Creator. He succeeded in getting a number of angels to side with him and failed in his efforts to stir up others (the elect) to take part in his attempt at dethroning the Most High. God, knowing of his plan, hurled him and his band from their place in heaven to the bottomless pit. It was at once a punishment of the wicked and an admonition to the other angels. Since with Lucifer his whole order had fallen, there was a gap in the heavenly host (9 orders instead of 10) which had to be filled. As all this happened before the creation of man, God thought of creating him as a substitute for the fallen order, that the saints, coming forth from man, might take, in heaven, the place of the apostates. Lucifer, by his rebellion turned Satan, though in the uttermost depths of the earth, was yet ("owing to his angelical nature") capable of rising to earth, even of entering Paradise. His hatred of God the victorious transferred itself to man, who had been created to replace him. He swore to avenge himself and he did so by causing Eve, and, through Eve, Adam, to eat of the forbidden fruit. They were thus driven from Paradise, robbed of their divine glory and hurled out into the vale of tears, this life. Sin has caused death and holds man in its grip, robbing earthly life of all its value. Satan is punished again; his tool, the serpent, is crippled and made deaf—but Satan's main aim was achieved. Man is fallen and thus in the power of Satan all his life. This miserable state of human affairs is made still more miserable by the unnatural vices of the angels, which cause the flood and sink the human race into a bottomless mire of evil. The only salvation possible is the belief in Jesus, who atones for human frailties. Authority for the story is Isaiah 14.12 and the working of the imagination, clustering round the theme. (cp. Beowulf I., about the origin of evil spirits, monsters and the like).

(F) Satan in Mohammedan Accounts

That Mohammed heard of this story or of part of it is evidenced by the fact that according to him too (contrary to the Jewish version) Satan had a definite personal reason for seducing man, viz.: the fact that he had been punished because of him. On refusing to worship Adam, he had become 'a stoned devil', Iblis had turned Satan, and it is thus natural that he swears an oath of revenge. Another reason for assuming that the author of the Koran— or at least its early commentators—had heard of the Lucifer motif, lies in the fact that Iblis according to Tabari and others, was a leading angel equalled by none in devotion, having charge over things between heaven and earth, as the treasurer of the garden of Eden. There are also some stories of his fortitude. Common to Christian and Mohammedan accounts of the story are the following features: (1) A prominent angel; (2) turns devil through disobedience; (3) finds himself injured by man; (4) hence seduces him. But the difference is very important. The Mohammedan angel (where the story is taken from Christian accounts) could disobey, but he could not rebel against God, he could never think of trying to dethrone Him and of placing himself on the throne in the uttermost north. At this point the two traditions clashed. The Christian conception of a rebellious angel was incompatible with the Jewish view, which has largely influenced Islamic lore. And Lucifer was defeated, and only some fragments of his story remain. Another difference, of course, lies in the fact that Iblis sins *after* the creation of man, whilst Lucifer does so *before* Adam is thought of, Lucifer's rebellion and overthrow being the cause of the creation of man.

In Jewish accounts (they all agree more or less with Genesis 3.1 ff) the serpent, an intelligent beast, endowed with speech and human passion, seduces Adam and Eve, either from sheer cunning malice, or because it lusted after Eve. There is no preceding story, leading up to the seduction. Even Martinus in his *Pugio Fidei* has only the story of Lucifer's disobedience, for Rabbi Moses ha-Darshan, upon whose Midrash Martinus's book is based, with all his love of foreign lore could not overcome his ingrained views of the absolute power of God and its absolute acknowledgment by the angels.[31] P.d.R.E. has

---

[31] *Pugio Fidei* (The Dagger of Faith) is a book "adversus Mauros et Judaeos", written by the monk Raymundus Martinus in the middle of the 13th century. It contains many passages "out of the great Genesis Rabba of R. Moses ha-Darshan", the genuineness of which has been doubted by some scholars, defended by others and is now finally established. See Neubauer, *Tobit XX f.*, and Epstein, in *Magazin für die Wissenschaft des Judentums*, 1888.

Rabbi Moses ha-Darshan lived in the first half of the eleventh century at Narbonne, then a city of Jewish learning. He was a great scholar and because of his homiletical skill was named "The Darshan". The unknown author of the Midrash Rabba Rabbeti used extensively the "Yesod", the opus of R. Moses, and Martini quoted from that Midrash, which had been fathered on R. Moses ha-Darshan. "Rabbi Moses ha-Darshan occasionally used foreign and unreliable sources in his commentaries and homi-

Samael, the enemy of Satan, but not on grounds similar to those of Lucifer; it corresponds rather to the passage in the Koran. Samael is thrown from heaven, the serpent loses his feet, master and servant receiving their punishment. Thus Lucifer does not exist outside Christian lore, but is prevalent enough in it, moving all through its early literature (the Christian Fathers) and through the middle ages towards its consummation in Milton's "Paradise Lost".[31a]

---

letical discussions; even such as disagreed in some points with Jewish traditional views. He believed the words of Eldad ha-Dani (a Jewish traveller of the ninth century, whose reports contain truth and fiction; see Epstein, *Eldad ha-Dani*), and used them to explain a passage in Proverbs. The author of the Midrash Rabba Rabbeti cited stories from Eldad introducing them with the words 'Our Rabbis have said'... In these stories there are some christological ideas as I have shown in my notes (p. 75), yet this did not prevent the author of that Midrash from citing them, for it appears that he found them in the work of Rabbi Moses ha-Darshan. For this reason the monk Raymundus Martinus used this Midrash in his '*Pugio Fidei*' and attributed it to Rabbi Moses..." Epstein, *Moses ha-Darshan*, Wien 1891, see also *Magazin*, 1888, p. 191f.

[31a] Gruenbaum sees the origin of the "fallen angels" in the phenomenon of shooting stars. He adduces as evidence P.d.R.E. ch. 7, where the following passage occurs: "All the Mazzikin (demons) which move in the firmament and the angels who fell from their holy place from heaven, when they ascend to hear the (divine) Word behind the veil, are pursued with a rod of fire, and return to their place." Friedlander (p. 46 and page 23, 5) does not mention the striking parallel in Moslem lore of Satan (or the Jinn) listening "behind the veil". Dr. A. Smythe Palmer, unaware of Gruenbaum's note, proposes the same origin as a new solution of the problem in the *Hibbert Journal* (1912), p. 766 ff., but he cites a great deal of new and important material, showing in detail how, among all Semites, the stars were associated with sin and "falling" (cp. also Baudissin's *Studien*). But Dr. Palmer goes too far in assuming e. g. that "He gave laws to them which they cannot transgress" implies moral laws for intelligent stars; it is a statement of their technical limits, i. e. they are bound to move in the course He has prescribed for them. Neither in Ps. 148.3 to be taken in any but a figurative sense, or we must postulate intelligent waters capable of speech. The passages quoted from the Hebrew Bible to show that "the idea that the heavenly bodies were intelligent and responsible servants of their creator was generally held by the Hebrews" do not at all convey the sense Dr. Palmer wishes to give them; not even Job 25.5 is conclusive. It is only later when the stars are identified, however vaguely, with angels and spirits that such notions prevail. That Zoroastrian influence is at work in this transformation is very likely, especially so since the Hebrew Bible has no notion of this sort and since Zoroastrianism has placed the Apocrypha and Christian lore under obligation (*ibidem*, p. 770). Samael's riding on the serpent has nothing to do with lightning (782, but see Luke, 10,18.).

Chapter 3.

SATAN

(A) Jewish Notions

Satan or the "Angel of Death" or "Samael" or "Ashmedai" are not the representatives of evil powers. They all appear as messengers of God, though occasionally misusing their power. It will suffice if I can bring evidence to the effect that good deeds were attributed to them. Kindness, consideration, delicacy of feeling—of all of these great gifts of heart Satan or the Angel of Death was said to be possessed. The difference in the conception of this angel is an essential one; it is of great importance for the comparative study of religions. The Mohammedan Iblis in this trait resembles the Christian Satan: there is no good will in him, but the Mohammedan Satan does not rebel.

Gen. Rabba 9: "Very good—that is the Angel of Death." "Very good—that is the Yezer Hara'." There are qualifying statements, however. In the case of the latter it is explained that the propagation of the human species is due to the sexual instinct, which, but for its necessity for the future of man, is evil.

As to the Angel of Death being "very good", R. Samuel b. Isaac explains his own dictum in the sense that the Angel of Death is a very necessary and wholesome institution, inasmuch as he destroys the sinner.

Satan, the Good One

Gen. Rabba 56: "The Angel of Death preserved Abraham, lest he die from the excitement resulting from the sacrifice of Isaac and its miraculous end."

Baba Batra 16a: "And Satan said to God: 'Lord of the Universe, I have gone to and fro in the whole world and have found none like Abraham, Thy servant. For Thou hadst told him, "Go walk about in the land, in its length and in its breadth, for to thee I shall give it," and when he wanted to bury Sarah he was unable to find a place to bury her, and yet he did not complain of Thy dealings with him'."

Abodah Zarah 20b: "The father of Samuel said, The Angel of Death told me: 'If I had not considered the dignity of man, I should have left open (visible) the place where I slaughter man (the throat)'."

Baba Batra 16a: "Rabbi Levi said: Satan and Peninah both acted for God's sake.[32] Satan saw that the Holy One blessed be He, was very fond of Job, so he said, 'He has perchance forgotten His love of Abraham'. Peninah, as it is said, 'And her rival grieved her to cause her to complain'."[33] When R. Aḥa bar Jacob reported this in Papunya, Satan came and kissed his feet.

Gittin 68f: Ashmedai shows genuine feeling when he weeps at the sight of a happy wedding party. "For,"— he explains to his companions—"the husband will be dead in three days and his wife will have to wait thirteen years for the levirate marriage!"

When Ashmedai's bulky figure becomes dangerous to a poor widow's hut, he twists his body, at her request, in order not to knock against it, and he does it so violently that he breaks a bone of his body, which gives him occasion for a good-natured jest. "This," he says, "serves to illustrate the proverb: 'Gentle words break the bone,'" i. e.

---

[32] Both had a good purpose when acting in an evil manner.

[33] i. e. that she pray to God. Hannah did so, her prayers were heard, and thus Peninah's work proved kindly.

by twisting his body to do as the widow gently asked him, he broke his bone.

The Angel of Death and R. Joshua Ben Levi

Babli Berakot 51a. The angel of death gives R. Joshua advice how to behave on various occasions.

Babli Ketub. 77a. He shows him his place in Paradise, and to save him fright, hands him his knife for a while.

In the Munich MS. the Angel of Death gives the Rabbi seven points of advice (see Dikduke Soferim *ad loc.*). A letter is sent by the same Rabbi from Paradise through the agency of the Angel of Death (Jellinek, Bet Hammidrasch II). These stories according to Jellinek (XIX f), who cites Josephus to support his theory, originated among the Essenes with whom our Rabbi had frequent dealings. But see A. Büchler, *Types of Jewish Palestinian Piety*, 1922.

Ibidem. The Angel of Death grants thirty days of grace to his friend, Rabbi Ḥanina b. Papa, so that the latter might go over his studies, to prepare "for the world to come with its academies."

Shabbat 32a: "Satan hath no power over two nations at the same time". For that reason R. Samuel would use the boat only when a non-Jew was present. The origin of this belief is quite clear. An angel can perform only *one* mission at a time (Gen. Rab.50). Satan, as an angel, can afflict one nation only (Yalkut Job 908). Again note the nearness in conception of Satan and the ordinary angel.

Yoma 67b, Levit. Rabba 21: The solar year has 365 days. The numerical value of השטן is 364. This indicates that all the days of the year Satan accuses, but on the Day of Atonement (Yom Kippur) he does not accuse.[34]

---

[34] Either because the he-goat appeases him, or because all Israel confess and repent on that day; also, because it is the Day of Atonement.

Midrash Psalm 27.3: Israel says to the Holy One blessed be He, "If the camp of Samael encamp against me, my heart shall not fear, for Thou hast assured me, 'On this day may Aaron enter the Sanctuary' (Levit. 16.3) without fear of Samael".

(B) According to Vendidad

Vendidad, Fargard XXII, verse 2–6 (translation of Fr. Spiegel, Leipzig 1852).

2. Ich, der ich Ahura-Mazda bin, ich der ich der Geber der Güter bin,

3. Als ich diese Wohnung schuf, die schöne, glänzende, sehenswürdige,[35]

4. (Sprechend) Ich will herausgehen, ich will hinübergehen.[36]

5. Da erblickte mich die Schlange Angramainyus.

6. Darauf machte die Schlange Angramainyus, der voll Tod ist, in Bezug auf mich neun Krankheiten und neunhundert und neuntausend und neun zehntausende.[37]

Vendidad XIX. Angramainyus (which is the serpent acc. to XXII) tries to deceive Zarathustra a to causend him to rebel against Ahura Mazda. But Zarathustra overcomes this temptation (v. 20–35), and now wishes to fight Angramainyus and to destroy the creation of the Daevas. He inquires of Ahura Mazda about these things and especially about the promises for pious souls after death.

The Daevas in consternation and helpless, unable to

---

[35] "Die Wohnung," acc. to Spiegel—the earth.
[36] "Agra mainyus erscheint auch im Bundehesch unter dieser Form."
[37] Spiegel considers this fargard to be late: "da ich durchaus solche Teile des Parsismus nicht für ursprünglich erachten kann, in welchen Ahura-Mazda gewissermassen von der Macht und dem Willen seiner eigenen Geschöpfe abhängig gedacht wird, wie dies im vorliegenden Capitel der Fall ist."

harm Zarathustra, fly into the depths of hell, into utter darkness.

Ibid. "Von der nördlichen[38] Gegend, von den nördlichen Gegenden stürzte Angramainyus hervor, er, der voll Tod ist, der Daeva der Daevas."[39]
On the Serpent as Enemy in the Vendidad, see *Z.D.M.G.* 11, 218 ff., article by R. Roth. Thraetaono and Trita (in Vedas) fight serpents and slay them.

(C) THE NEW SATAN

An altogether different Satan appears in the books of the New Testament. Here he is wholly wicked, destitute of any relieving trait, such as Jewish folk-lore has endowed him with; he is the very principle of evil. But even in the New Testament he is not represented as originally wicked. The background of this new Satan is a mosaic of many colors and materials; for its biblical evidence it rests upon the misinterpreted passage of Isaiah 14, 12, with which I have dealt more fully in the chapter on Lucifer. According to the legend based upon that interpretation, there was an angel of rare beauty and excellence, called Lucifer, who was led astray by his splendor, became arrogant, rebelled against his master, God, and fell from heaven. From the moment of his fall he became Satan. Originally a rebel against the authority of God, he becomes the princi-

---

[38] This might be of importance. צפון might then be due to Persian influence. Apakhudara is the northern region, from which the Daevas come and whither they fly from before the prayers of the Mazdayaeans. As to the North in Mythology, see K. Helm, *Mythologie*: Joetunheimr (hell?) lies in the North. The Daevas live in the North (Vend. Fargard II, 10; VII, 2; XIX). Darmesteter in the Introduction in Vendidad S.B.O.E. considers Jewish influence on the Mazdean Genesis as not impossible. P. d. R. E. 3, "From the North darkness goes forth into the world. There is the abode of destroying spirits, demons, etc." Yalkuṭ Reubeni (ad Gen. 4): The Serpent thought: "Because Eve's soul is from the North (of the North) מצפון, I shall be able to persuade her to sin". Pseudo-Ephraem V: The Antichrist will come from Dan in the North (Dan's emblem was the Serpent).

[39] It is worth while to consider whether this may not be the origin of Satan's = Samael's = Azazel's kingship over demons, devils, etc.

pal rebel against Him, the representative of the second empire, opposed to God. He remains God's deliberate, implacable and consistent opponent, until his final overthrow.

Gregory, *Moralia*, XXXIV, adduces Ecclesiasticus 10, 23 as evidence of his interpreration of Isaiah 14, 12, from which the equation Lucifer = Satan is derived. The passage in Ecclesiasticus reads: "Pride is the beginning of all sin." The Hebrew text has (Peters 343): כי מקוה זדון חטא ומקורה יביע זמה. "For the sin is the rallying place of insolence, and its source overfloweth with depravity." Perhaps we should read מקור and transpose כי מקור חטא זדון.

With Lucifer fell a number of his fellow angels, who had been his fellow conspirators. Hence Satan occasionally appears with his wicked host.

"Everlasting fire is prepared for the devil and his angels." Matthew 25. 41.

"Since the demons and apostate spirits are at his service, the devil performs wonders through them by the working of magic." Irenaeus—*Against Heresies* (Ante-Nicene Christian Fathers, IX), p. 129.

He has been punished for his rebellion. "And the great dragon was cast down, the old serpent, he that is called Devil and Satan, the deceiver of the whole world." Revelation 12, 9: "And when the thousand years are finished, Satan shall be loosed out of prison". This is the less severe version of Revelation 20, 7, as compared with Matthew 25. 41. But he has apparently come up again. Hence the comfort, "And the God of peace shall bruise Satan under your feet shortly." Romans, 12. 9. Cp. Genesis 3, 1 ff. Satan is held responsible for every act of wickedness. "And Satan entered into Judas, called Iscariot." Luke 20, 3. Cp. *ibidem* 20, 8. See also Note 225.

Gregory, *Moralia*, Preface, 8: "In putting forth his strength against Job, the enemy entered the lists against God, and in this way blessed Job, the intermediate subject of the contest between God and Devil." Contrast as probably a case of parallel lore: 11.38, "In his work he obeys God's decrees." ii.15, "Satan can do nothing without God."

The Devil and his Angels

Origen, *De Principiis*, Preface 6. "Regarding the devil and his angels, and the opposing influences, the teaching of the Church has laid down that these beings exist indeed; but what they are, or how they exist, it has not explained with sufficient clearness. This opinion, however, is held by most that the Devil was an angel and that, having become an apostate, he induced as many as possible of the angels to fall away with himself, and these up to the present time are called his angels."[40]

Ibidem I.8. Angels are capable of good and of evil.

Justin Martyr, *Apol.* 27, "With us the Prince of the evil spirits is called a serpent and Satan and the devil...He will be sent into fire with his host, there to be tormented unto endless eternity."

Conflicting Traditions

The Devil once Good. Origen, *De Princ.*, I.8: "There was once a time when he (the devil) was good, when he walked in the paradise of God between the Cherubim."

Satan's Envy. Ephraem 50. 4. "The wicked one envied men's greatness. He envied Adam and his children."

---

[40] This must be taken to refer either to "Lucifer" or to the episode based on Genesis 4. 4. The Devil seems to have been unattended by anyone when thrown from heaven as a punishment for seducing Adam.

"A great elevation did God ordain for man that fleshly creatures might ascend and be spiritual like the angels on high. In all degrees did the Good One lift them up, by all devices did the wicked one bring them down."

XXXVIII, 3. "Satan is the Evil Principle which God hates."

Satan. Gregory, *Moralia*, II.4: "How could Satan come before God?"[41] "How could Satan be present among the elect angels, he who had a long time before been damned and banished from their number, as his pride required?[42]

"Yet he is well described as having been present among them; for though he lost his blessed estate, yet he did not part with a nature like to theirs, and though his deserts sink him, he is lifted up by the properties of his subtle nature.[43]

"He came before God, but he did not see the Lord. He was in the Lord's sight, but the Lord was not in his. Because even those very things which flee from God's face cannot be hidden, in that all things are naked to the view of the Most High; Satan being absent came to Him who was present."

Luke 10.18. Jesus himself interprets Isaiah 14 in the Lucifer sense: "I saw Satan like lightning from heaven." But that again may be independent of the text, like the examples shown before.

The Devil in the Apocalypse is identified with "the angel of the bottomless pit", "the dragon", the old serpent: he fights the Archangel (Apocal. 19.12).

This is reminiscent of the Babylonian stories of the fight between Marduk and Tiamat.

---

[41] Gregory has the N. T. Satan in mind. Satan in the Hebrew Bible is an angel like any other; see above.

[42] That is due to the "Lucifer" interpretation of the famous passage in Isaiah.

[43] Again the traditions as against the text produce a dilemma.

Chapter 4

OBJECTION TO THE CREATION OF MAN

(A) in Jewish Literature

Gen. Rabba 8, 5. Rabbi Simon (4th cent., Bacher s. n.) said: "In the hour when the Holy One blessed be He came to create the first man, the ministering angels formed themselves into parties[44] and companies.[45] Some said: 'Let him be created', others:'Let him not be created'. To this division Psalm 85.11 refers: 'Kindness and Truth are met together. Righteousness and Peace have kissed each other'. Kindness said: 'Let him be created, for he is a bestower of loving-kindnesses'. Truth said: 'Let him not be created, for he is falsehood.' Justice said; 'Let him be created, for he deals justly'. Peace said: 'Let him not be created, for he is wholly quarrelsome'.

"What did the Holy One blessed be He? He took Truth and cast it to the earth. The ministering angels said before the Holy One blessed be He: 'Lord of the Universe! Art Thou despising Thy chief of ceremonies?[46] Let Truth come up from the earth'. To this refers (ibid. 12): 'Let Truth spring out of the earth'.[47] The angels said before the Holy One blessed be He: 'Lord of the Universe! What is mortal man that Thou art mindful of him, and the son of the earthborn that Thou visitest him? (Psalm 8.5) He

---

[44] The whole story is probably based on נעשה, which implies cousultation. Therefore it was interpreted as consultation with the various parties of the angels.

[45] It is important to note that some angels are in favor of the creation of man, and that objection to his creation is followed by worship of Adam. It is interesting to find that Satan raises no objection: he is not even mentioned here. God does not require angels even to bow to Adam (see Koran); they do it on their own account.

[46] So Jastrow, who is inclined to explain אוטכסיא = טכסים על chief of ceremonies; cp. Shabb. 31 a. According to Rashi, the word means 'seal', while Theodor thinks of ἀλήθεια (the angel of) Truth.

[47] This is an excellent type of Midrash. The fact that the one sentence follows the other, is made to account for the story. It also accounts for the division. Why has אמת to spring from the ground, while צדק may look down from above? Probably צדק pleased God, while אמת displeased Him by opposing His plan.

will cause us anguish'.[48] He said to them: 'If so, why (for what purpose) were sheep and oxen, all of them, why were the fowl of the heavens and the fish of the sea created? A tower full of all good without guests, what profit has the owner from filling it?' Then they said: 'Lord of the Universe, O Lord our God, how glorious is Thy name in all the earth. Do what pleases Thee'."

Numb. Rabba 19.3—Gen. Rabba 17.5. "When the Holy One blessed be He desired to create man, He took counsel with the ministering angels. He said to them: 'Let us make man in our image'. They replied:[49] 'What is mortal man, that Thou art mindful of him?' (Psalm 8.5). He said: 'Man, whom I wish to create—his wisdom is greater than yours'. What did He do? He gathered all cattle, beasts, and birds, caused them to pass before them and said: 'What are their names?' They knew not. As soon as He had created man (Adam), He caused them to pass before him, asking: 'What are their names?' He said: 'This it is fitting to call "ox" and this "lion" and this "ass" and this "camel" and this "eagle", as it is said: 'And he called names'. God said to him: 'What is thy name?' He said: 'Adam'. (Why?) 'Because I was created from the earth (Adamah)'. God asked: 'What is My name?' He said: 'Adonai, because Thou art Lord of all creatures. As it is said: I am Lord, that is My name (Isaiah 42.8), i. e. this is the name the first man gave Me'."

Babli Sanhedrin 38b. Judah in the name of Rab,[50] said: "When the Holy One blessed be He desired to create man, He created a party of ministering angels. He said to them: 'Is it your wish that we create man in our image?' They said: 'What is mortal man that Thou art mindful of him, and

---

[48] Or: "Why has this trouble been created?" reading with Theodor *ad locum*.
[49] Some of the angels are punished for their objection, see Sanh. 38b for details.
[50] Judah lived in the 3rd century; he was one of the most prominent pupils of the great Rab. See Bacher, *A. B. A.*, 47f.

the son of the earthborn that Thou visitest him?' He stretched forth His little finger between them and burned them.

"Thus also the second group. The third said to Him: 'Lord of the Universe, what did the former ones avail in speaking before Thee? All the world is Thine, whatever Thou desirest to do in Thy work, do it.. When He reached the men of the generation of the separation[51] and the generation of the flood, whose dealings were corrupt, they (the angels) said to Him: 'Have the former (groups of angels) not spoken rightly?' He said to them: 'Even to old age I am the same, even to grey hairs I will carry you'" (Isaiah 46.4).

Pirke de R. Eliezer XI. "The Holy One blessed be He, spoke to the Torah: 'Let us make man in our image, according to our likeness'. The Torah spoke before Him: 'Sovereign of all world! This man whom Thou wouldst create will be limited in his days and full of anger, and he will come into the power of sin. Unless Thou wilt be longsuffering with him, it will be well for him not to have come into the world'. The Holy One blessed be He rejoined: 'And is it for naught that I am called slow to anger and abounding in mercy?'"

See also Midrash Haggadah, Genesis, 126: Rabbi Berachia said: "When the Holy One blessed be He came to create the first man, He saw the righteous and the wicked descending from him. He thought: 'If I create him, the wicked shall rise from him; (but) if I should not create him, how can the righteous arise from him?' What did God do? He put away the way of the wicked from before Him and joined to it the measure of mercy and created him (man), as it is said: 'For God favours the way of the righteous, but the way of the ungodly shall perish' (Psalm 1.6). What

---
[1] Which witnessed the separation of races, Genesis 11.

does תאבד mean? He destroyed it from before Him, joined to it the measure of mercy and created him (man)." Rabbi Hanina puts it thus: "When the Holy One blessed be He came to create the first man he took counsel with the ministering angels. He said to them: 'Let us make man'. They answered: 'What is his nature?' He replied: 'Righteous men will rise from him'. To this refers: 'For God knows the way of the righteous', i. e. God made known to the ministering angels the way of the righteous. 'But the way of the wicked perishes'. He destroyed them from before Him, for had He discovered unto them that the wicked will rise from him, then the measure of justice would not have permitted that man be created."

General Remarks

Satan does not "exist" at the time of the creation, or if he does, he raises no objection. The angels who object do so in the interest of God's plan, desirous of preventing future evil. This story may be taken to refer to the time either preceding or following the "Fall of Lucifer". The angels created on the second day would, before the sixth, object to the creation of Man. "Lucifer" must have fallen between the second and the fifth day. A faint reminiscence of his fall, as interpreted in the "Ersatztheorie",[52] is the Caliphate of man in the Koran. According to Jewish ideas 'Ersatztheorie' has no sense. The Universe was created because of Israel; Israel because of the Torah (cp. Rashi. Gen. 1.1). Man is the center of all things. The question of where the "Ersatztheorie" comes from will be treated more fully in the chapter on "Lucifer".

Midrash Abkir[53], cited in Yalkut *ad Genesis* 6. 4. "Rabbi

---

[52] According to this theory, God created man as a substitute for the fallen angels who had revolted against Him. The Christian Fathers make much of it. The German word is briefer than any English translation I could think of.

[53] A Midrash extant in quotations on Genesis and Exodus. All the homilies ended with אמן בימינו כן יהי רצון; hence the name. It was cited as early as the 11th century.

Joseph was asked by his pupils: "What is Azazel?" He said: "When the generation of the deluge arose and worshipped idols, the Holy One blessed be He was grieved. Immediately two angels, Shamhazai and Azazel,[54] arose and said before him: 'Lord of the Universe, have we not said before Thee, when Thou createdst Thy world: What is mortal that Thou be mindful of him?'" (See Jellinek, Bet Hammidrasch, IV, 127).

The antiquity of this story is established not only by the fact that the Talmud, Genesis and Numbers Rabba introduce it, but also by the following consideration.

Rabbi Akiba expressed what generations before him must have felt. He emphasized the importance of every letter in the Bible; the importance of every word had been taken for granted. Every incident has to tell its tale, every suffix, every singular and plural. And especially such syllables, words and phrases as apparently are superfluous. Now, in Genesis 1.26, God says: "Let *us* make man".[55]— "Us", where "Me" would have been sufficient. Why then "us"? He obviously consulted somebody. And now the door is open for all kinds of suggestion, theories and stories. Whom would the Holy One consult? Of course, the angels. It is clear, then, He consulted angels before creating man. What would they say? Would they be unanimous or not? Are there objections that could well be brought forward on such an occasion? Thus works the soul and mind of the people. There are household words which will come into play. Hence David's despondent cry, "What is mortal man that Thou shouldst be mindful of

---

[54] On Shamhazai see M. Schwab, *Vocab. d'Angélologie*, who tries to identify the name with עזא.

[55] The Church Fathers also comment on this point. Gregorius Nyssenus, *On Creation*, page 16, and Justin Martyr, *Dial. cum Tryph*. c. 62, adduce this sentence as evidence for the Trinity, but the objection to this explanation by Jewish scholars is cited. Ber. Rabba 8, 5: "While the angels debate, man is created. God says: 'Why do you dispute? Adam is made already.'"

him?" Who will bring that forward? And who on the other side will speak for man? Upon occasion, in a haggadic discourse, Psalm 85. 11–12 is connected with Psalm 8. 5–6. The connection is obvious, the story gains in detail. And now when these verses are put together, they tell the whole tale.

"What is man, that Thou art mindful of him?
And the son of man, that Thou thinkest of him?
Mercy and truth are met together:
Righteousness and peace have kissed each other."

That gives the action. The sentences refer to the consultation in heaven previous to the creation of man. Mercy and Truth have met. Mercy of course will be for him. But Truth will bring forward his failings. Peace will oppose him, for he engenders strife. Righteousness pleads his cause, looking at his good deeds (Gen. Rabba 8. 5).

Will God be persuaded by them? Certainly not. For He is above all angels and His plan must not be interfered with. And then, what could be the meaning of the next clause:

"Truth springs out of the earth;
And Righteousness has looked down from Heaven."

This also appears now in the new, dramatic light. Truth, in punishment for its objection, has been cast down from heaven, but, being Truth, it springs up again out of the earth. Righteousness, having commended God's plan, remains on high. In the same manner does popular imagination weave a story out of the following verses. The angels having (in verses 5, 6 and 7) objected to man, God replied (in verse 8):

"Sheep and oxen all of them,
Yea, and the beasts of the field."

What reply is this? Obviously He says: "Do you not perceive? All has been created, and if there be no man to enjoy it, why all the trouble of calling it into existence? 'Of what avail a larder full of dainties, if there be no guests to enjoy them?'" The angels, overcome by this argument, then say:

"O Lord, our Lord,
How glorious is Thy Name in all the earth!"

"No", someone objects, "so easily must no one get off who opposed God!" And to please him the angels are burned—one group, a second one. The third agrees, and man is created.

So much about the psychology of the story. Pirke de Rabbi Eliezer has a different version. The Torah objects. This is Hellenistic thought. Wisdom, Logos, and thus Torah. Wisdom, which (Proverbs 3.19 and 8.22) took part in the creation, is the Torah which was ready thousands of years before man was created. Torah is appeased by a sentence of her own, "O Lord, Lord, God compassionate and merciful" (Exodus 34.6). All these details are woven by the Jewish genius unadulterated by foreign influence. Angels are an important factor in heaven. They are sent to man by God. They visit Abraham, save Isaac, lead Moses and the people on the way to the Holy Land.

With the progress of time the simple story receives additions, which cluster round its skeleton. God, on that occasion, communicates His whole plan concerning man. He concealed from the angels man's failings. The objecting bands are those of Michael, Gabriel (these two alone are saved from destruction) and Labbiel, whose troop, on his advice, agree. His name is changed to Raphael (Root: Rafa—to heal) because he had saved his band by his advice to comply and thus to escape ruin.

(B) In Mohammedan Sources

Koran 11. 28–31. "When the Lord said unto the angels: 'I am going to place a substitute on earth', they said: 'Wilt Thou place there one who[56] will do evil therein, and shed blood? But we celebrate Thy praise and sanctify Thee'. God answered: 'Verily I know that which ye know not'. And He taught Adam the names of all things and then proposed them to the angels, and said: 'Declare unto Me the names of these things if you say truth'. They answered: 'Praise be unto Thee, we have no knowledge but what Thou teachest us, for Thou art knowing and wise'. God said: 'Adam, tell them their names', and when he had told them their names, God said: 'Did I not tell you that I know the secrets of heaven and earth, and know that which ye discover and that which ye conceal?'"[57]

This part, as may be seen from a comparison with the Jewish sources, is entirely Jewish, free from any Christian coloring. It is natural for Mohammed to add: "and who will shed blood", for murder is one of the three cardinal sins he often refers to (cp. the Zohra legend: The angels agree to commit murder after having drunk wine, in order that Zohra may comply with their adulterous request). A comparison with the Jewish texts will show that according to them there were some angels in favor of the creation, some bands entirely against it, and the rest entirely for it. According to both accounts the angels have moral reasons for opposing the creation of man. The Jewish texts have it that they are punished for their objection. Mohammed mentions nothing about that.

Tabari *ad locum:* "When the angels said: 'Wilt

---

[56] The Jinn who had lived on earth before man commit these sins. As (Isaiah 14. 12) Satan fell from heaven *before* the creation of man—(hence the theory of substitution: man created in lieu of fallen Satan and his companions)—there is apparently a connection between these legends.

[57] Cp. the Jewish accounts.

Thou place there one who will do evil therein and shed blood?' God sent a fire and burned them. And when Iblis saw what punishment had come down on his kinsfolk, he went up to heaven and stayed with the angels, until God created Adam and then came His command to worship Adam, and his rebellion".

Compare this with the story in Tabari 1, 83, according to which some angels are burned for refusing to worship Adam. Here they are burned for objecting to the creation. There are two cycles of legends: the one dealing with the objection to the creation on the part of some angels, of which the original may be found in Sanhedrin; the other of Satan's refusal to worship Adam, which is extra-talmudic and Christian.[58] Mohammed and the fathers of Moslem tradition confused the two, and it is from looking at the remains of these independent accounts that we are able to reconstruct the whole in its original form.

It is very interesting to find the origin of the Ibl's theory (that he was a Jinn, not an angel) in Augustine, *Enchiridion* 28. It is very likely that the Christian informant of Mohammed knew and told him what Augustine said, viz: "Certain angels through impious *pride* deserted God and were cast down from their high heavenly habitation into the lowest darkness of this air; but that number of angels which was left continued in eternal blessedness with God, and in holiness. For the rest of the angels were not descended from the one who fell and was condemned, that original evil might bind them, as in the case of man, with the chains of succession subject to it and draw down all to deserved punishment". This theory could not have come from Jewish sources, for there is no indication of Satan being different in descent from other angels, while Samael comes into "history" only after the creation of

[58] Cp. *Schatzhöhle*, ch. 5.

man. The curious tale of Adam and Eve, during the years of separation, propagating their species with male and female demons, is nowhere used to account for the existence of Samael, who is the Babylonian popular edition of Satan.

Tabari 1. 85: "On the authority of Ibn Abbas it is told that the angels objected to the creation of man on account of what they had observed regarding the affairs of the Jinn. Iblis, a Jinn, had been a most devout worshipper of God in heaven, whither he had come when his kinsfolk had been burned, and he rebelled when God commanded him to worship Adam."

Tabari has another story, coming from the Zohra-Istahar cycle, according to which Iblis was for a thousand years a just judge over the Jinn on earth where they lived before Adam. Because of his just reign the name "authority" was bestowed upon him; on account of this he became puffed up with pride, etc.

I have been unable to find any genuine Christian traditions relating to any objection to the creation of man on the part of angels. It appears that Sale's note to Sura II, 33 (mentioning Irenaeus, Lactantius and Gregory of Nyssa as authorities for the tale) is unjustified. "This occasion of the Devil's fall has some affinity with an opinion which has been pretty much entertained among Christians, that the angels being informed of God's intention to create man after His own image, etc., some of them thinking their glory to be eclipsed thereby, envied man's happiness and so revolted."

Satan's Oath of Revenge
(Koran)

Sura VII, 15 (Sale's translation). "He (the devil) said: 'Because thou hast depraved me, I will lay wait for men in Thy strait way; then will I come upon them from before and from behind and from their right hands and from their left; and shall not find the greater part of them thankful.'[59] God said unto him: 'Get thee hence, despised and driven (far away).'[60] The Devil replied (Sura XV, 20f): 'O Lord, because Thou hast seduced me, I will surely tempt them (to disobedience) in the earth. And I will seduce them all except such of them as shall be Thy chosen servants.' (God) said: 'This is the right way with Me. Verily as to My servants,[61] thou shalt have no power over them; but over those only who shall be seduced and who shall follow thee.[62]'"

Sura XVIII, 64. "When we said unto the angels, 'Worship Adam', they all worshipped him except Iblis, who said, 'Shall I worship him whom Thou hast created of clay?' And he said: 'What thinkest Thou as to this man whom Thou hast honored above me? Verily if Thou grant me respite until the day of Resurrection, I will extirpate his offspring, except a few.' God answered: 'Begone!'"

Sura XXXVIII (near end). God said: "Get thee hence, therefore, for thou shalt be driven away (from mercy)"...

Iblis said: "By Thy might (do I swear), I will surely seduce them all except Thy servants who shall be peculiarly chosen from among them."

God said: "It is a just sentence. And I speak the truth:

[59] It is mainly envy which caused his fall and it is his fall which now causes his vengeful oath. Cp. this with the other accounts.

[60] But in Sura XV God agrees with Satan's plan. I should not like to press the texts too closely, or I should have said: Sura CVII expresses the Christian antagonism, Satan, the power for evil, hated by God; Sura XV the Jewish view, Satan sent by God to test man, to punish the wicked and weak and to acknowledge the virtue of men like Job.

[61] Cp. Shabbat 146a, Yeb. 103b. "Why are idolaters lascivious? Because they stood not on Mount Sinai. For when the Serpent came in (Cp. Rashi on הישׁיאני) unto Eve he infected her (and through her the human race) with lasciviousness. Israel's sensual passions ceased (through the influence of religion) because they stood on Mount Sinai. The sensuality, however, of the idol worshippers was not removed because they did not stand on Mount Sinai." Cp. also the גמטריה of השׂטן = 364. See Lev. Rabba 21

[62] Cp. Job 1.6. Some such agreement seems to be expressed here.

I will surely fill hell with thee and with such of them as shall follow thee, altogether."

Adam in Paradise and Satan's Second Fall

(Jewish Accounts)

Genesis Rabba 8.10: Rabbi Hosea (Bacher, *APA*, I. 92) said: "When the Holy One blessed be He created the first man, the angels mistook him and wished to say 'Holy' before him. What does this resemble? It is like unto a king and his Eparch[63] who were in a carriage and the people of the province wished to say 'My lord' to the king, but knew not which (of the two) was the king. What did the king do? He pushed and threw the viceroy from the carriage, then they knew the king. Thus, when the Holy One blessed be He had created the first man, the angels mistook him. What did He do? He caused sleep to fall on him and all knew that he was but man. To this refers Isaiah 2.22: 'Cease ye from man, in whose nostrils is a breath; for how little is he to be accounted.'"

Sanhedrin 49b: Rabbi Judah[64] said: "The first man was sitting in the garden of Eden, and the ministering angels were roasting meat and cooling[65] wine for him. The serpent looked at him, saw his honor and envied him."

Pirke de Rabbi Eliezer 2: "All the creatures saw him and became afraid of him, thinking that he was their creator, and they came to prostrate themselves before him. Adam said to them: 'What is this, ye creatures? Why are ye come to prostrate yourselves before me? Come, I and you, let us adorn in majesty and might, and acclaim as king over us the One who created us.'"

---

[63] This word is important for the light it throws on the history of the exegesis of Genesis 41.43. Eparch = Viceroy.

[64] In Abot de Rabbi Nathan, 1, the story is related in the name of Rabbi Judah ben Bathyra.

[65] Reading: מצני. The other reading is מסנין, and means 'filter'.

Pirke de Rabbi Eliezer 13: "The ministering angels stood before the Holy One blessed be He, saying: 'Sovereign of all worlds! What is man that Thou shouldst take notice of him?' God said: 'Are you able to stand up and call the names of all the creatures which I have created?' They stood up, but were unable. Forthwith Adam stood up and called the names. When the ministering angels saw this they retreated and said: 'If we do not take counsel against this man, that he sin before his Creator, we cannot prevail against him.'"[66]

(Christian Account)

"Schatzhöhle",[67] edited by Bezold, p. 5: "When the angels saw his splendid appearance, they were moved by the fairness of his aspect. And God gave him there the dominion over all creatures, and all the wild beasts and the cattle and the birds, and they came before Adam and he gave them names, and they bowed their heads before him and worshipped him, and all their natures worshipped and served him. And the angels and powers heard the voice of God, who said to him, 'O Adam, behold I have made thee king, priest, prophet, lord, head and leader of all creatures and they serve thee and are thine.[68] And I

[66] According to Gen. R. 17, 4 (R. Aha, who tells this story, lived in the 4th century, Bacher, *APA* III, 106f), the angels object also, but on seeing Adam's achievement they are silent. Nowhere in genuinely Jewish lore are they thought of as capable of passions This shows at once the antiquity of Gen. R. and the late date of Pirke d. R.E See Theodor's article in the *Jewish Encyclopædia*, s. v. The final redaction of Genesis Rabba took place about 450 c. E., most of the material belonging to the third to fifth century. According to Friedlander, *l. c.*, the date of the final redaction of Pirke de R. E. is either the second or the third decade of the ninth century. "This late date does not however indicate that most of the material at the disposal of the redactor did not belong to a much earlier period. Some legends go back to the third and even to the first century." See also *Pugio*, 558 and Pesikta, Parah. Satan's subsequent action is then determined by his jealousy of man (because Adam knew the names or because of his honor), or because he lusted after Eve, or because of his oath of revenge. Unable to harm God, he harms His creatures.

[67] The Schatzhöhle (מערת גזא) is an original Syriac work, anonymous, which dates probably from the sixth century. It consists of an expansion of the early biblical history, somewhat after the manner of the Book of Jubilees. See Lagarde, *Mitteilungen*, III (1889), pp. 49–79, IV, 1891, pp. 6–16.

[68] This exaggeration of Adam's greatness is Christian. Cp. the opposite tendency in Talmud and Midrash.

have given thee dominion over all I have created.' And when the angels heard this word, they all bent their knees and worshipped him.

"And when the head of the lower order saw that greatness had been given to Adam, he envied him thenceforth, refused to worship him and said to his powers: 'Worship him not and praise him not with the angels. It befits him to worship me, not me to worship dust, formed out of a grain of dust.' Such things the rebel had uttered and was disobedient[69] and by his own free will became separated from God. And he was felled and he fell, he and his whole band. On the sixth day in the second hour, he fell from heaven, and they were stripped of the robes of their glory, and his name was called Satana,[70] because he had turned away from God, and Sheda, because he had been cast down,[71] and Daiva,[72] because he had lost the robe of his glory. And look, from that same day and until today, he and all his armies are stripped and naked and ugly to look on. And after Satan had been cast from Heaven, Adam was exalted so that he ascended to Paradise."

Vita Adae 13.1: "The devil replied: It is for thy sake that I have been hurled from that place. When thou wast formed, I was hurled out of the presence of God and banished from the company of the angels. Michael also brought thee and made us worship thee in the sight of God. And God the Lord spake: 'Here is Adam', and Michael went out and called all the angels, saying, 'Worship the image of God as the Lord God has commanded.' And Michael himself worshipped first, then he called me and

---

[69] Cp. 'and he became infidel' of the Koran.

[70] Hebrew שטה. For an interesting parallel see Recanati, Lev. 19, p. 148a.

[71] Connecting it with שדא, the Syr. is שדא acc. to Zimmern, from Assyr. šêdu (demon).

[72] This is the Vendidad daeva. The connection with על דאובד לבושה is as faulty as popular etymology can be. Daeva contains אבד in different order. דוה 'unclean' would have been more plausible. Perhaps דיוא may give a clue.

said: 'Worship the image of God the Lord.' And I said, 'I have no need to worship Adam. I will not worship an inferior and younger being. I am his senior in the creation. It is his duty to worship me'[73] (15,1; 2). When the angels who were under me heard this they refused to worship him, and Michael said, 'Worship the image of God. But if thou wilt not worship him, the Lord God will be wroth with thee', and I said, 'If He will be wroth with me, I will set my seat above the stars of heaven and will be like the Highest'[74] (16.1ff.). And God the Lord was wroth with me and banished me and my angels from our glory. And on thy account we were expelled and hurled down. And we were grieved when we saw thee in such joy and glory. And with guile I cheated thy wife and caused thee to be expelled through her from the joy and luxury as I have been driven out of my glory."

(Mohammedan Accounts)

Koran II, 32: "And when we said unto the angels, 'Worship Adam', they all worshipped him except Iblis,[75] who refused and was puffed up with pride and became of the number of unbelievers."

Who is Iblis? Tabari, History, I, 78, 166 (condensed):

[73] Cp. P. d. R. E. 13.

[74] He has his bands, he has his troupe, and from refusing to obey God's order, he proceeds to challenge His authority.

[75] Iblis, apparently *Diabolos*, shortened either because the word was too long for the Arabic rule of three radicals or—this is a suggestion of Dr. J. E. Thomas of the University Library at Cambridge—because 'Di' might have been taken as the Aramaic relative pronoun. Cp. the Arabic for 'Alexander' (Al-Iskander). Iblis is identified with Satan (Sura VII, 22). From the text one should infer that Iblis was an angel, for "When we said unto the *angels*, 'Worship Adam', all worshipped except Iblis." On the other hand there is the Mohammedan conception—borrowed from the Jews—of obedient angels. We find therefore the commentators busy explaining that Iblis was not an angel, at least not a regular one.—(Etymology according to Moh. Comment. from the root بلس despair, صفرة وابلاس yellowness and despair; it thus means (a) despair of good and repentance, (b) despair of sorrow and evil, (c) deprived. For Iblis deprived himself of any virtue he previously possessed by becoming a cursed Satan) · As for الا one might deprive it of its force by referring to the exception called متصل ; according to the grammarians, الا may exclude a thing not included. See Wright, *Arabic Grammar*, 2, § 186 B. C.

"God had made him beautiful and refined him and enthroned him over the lower heavens and earth. His name was Iblis. He made him one of the treasurers of Paradise, but he was puffed up with pride against his master, claimed the supreme authority, and summoned all who were before him to worship him. And God transformed him into a stoned[76] devil, and made him ugly and stripped from him what he had granted him and cursed him and drove him from heaven immediately, together with his adherents, to the fire of hell. Iblis was of a very glorious tribe. According to Ibn Abbas he was of a tribe of angels called Jinn.[77] They were created from the flaming fire.[78]"

Ibn Abbas, p. 81: "The Jinn were created from the 'fire clear from smoke'. All the angels were created from light, except this angel.[79] The first to inhabit the earth were the Jinn and they did evil therein and shed blood and killed one another. And God sent Iblis against them with an army of angels, and this was the tribe who are called Jinn. And Iblis and his followers fought them until he drove them into the islands of the sea and the sides of the mountains.[80] And when Iblis had done so, he became puffed up with pride and was beguiled by himself and said, 'I have accomplished a thing which none has accomplished.'"[81]

---

[76] Satan was stoned when eavesdropping at the door of the heavens to hear the mysteries which were told to the angels.

[77] *Jinn* from the root جنّ (1) 'to overshadow', (2) 'to conceal' by overshadowing. Iblis one of the treasurers of Paradise, see also Gruenbaum, *l. c.*, p. 291.

[78] Hence his proud 'Shall I, created of fire, bow to the clay form?' Ibn Abbas is by no means reliable. See Sprenger, *Das Leben und die Lehre des Mohammed*, I, 17 ff. II, 106 f.; also *Encyclopedia of Islam, s. v.*

[79] Tab. I, 179 adduces another reason why Iblis was no real angel. Angels, according to Mohammedan views, are unable to propagate their species. Iblis as the father of all devils and demons, cannot be an angel. All these explanations are necessary because Iblis has sinned whereas angels are impeccable. Iblis also is passionate, while angels know no passion.

[80] The Daevas too are driven back to the mountains of the North.

[81] This is an exact parallel to Lucifer, originally an archangel, then puffed up with pride. Here however, Iblis becomes arrogant from a single achievement. Ibn Abbas denies that the tribe of Iblis was created from fire like all other angels. The angels were created from light, Iblis and his tribe from 'fire clear like smoke' (Tab. 81). The details, as e. g. treasurership and dominion over lower heavens, are pure Moslem lore.

The following appears to be borrowed from the Christian accounts of Lucifer. It is not a particular cause of pride, but his general excellence and high rank which incite Iblis to revolt. On the authority of Ibn Abbas: "Iblis was the king of the lower heavens and their manager, and he was treasurer of Paradise.

"He marvelled at himself, seeing that he had excellence[82] therein, and he became puffed up with pride against his Master, mighty and glorious."

Ibn Abbas (Tab. 83): "Before Iblis undertook to rebel with the angels his name was Azazel and he was among the inhabitants of the earth.[83] And he was one of the angels strongest in devotion and noblest in knowledge. Thus he was incited to pride. He was of a tribe called Jinn. Iblis was of the remnant of the creatures whom God had created, to whom God had given the command which they disobeyed" (this may be a reminiscence of Gen. 6. 1–4).

Ibn Abbas: "God created man and said to the angels, 'Worship Adam', and they said, 'We shall not do so', and God sent a fire against them and burned them.[84] Then he created these angels, and He said, 'Will ye not worship Adam?' They said, 'Yes'. And Iblis was one of those who refused to worship Adam."

[82] According to Moses Ibn Harun, Iblis said: "God has given me this excellence only on account of my excellence." According to Amr Ibn Hammad, Iblis' pride was a direct cause of God's intention to put a deputy on earth, just as (see Aelfric) Lucifer's sin diminished God's ten legions by one and caused Him to consider the creation of man as a substitute for the fallen order.

[83] With this agrees his name 'tiller of the ground', حارث. This statement is not uninfluenced by the Jinn tradition.

[84] In Sanhedrin 38b this burning incident occurs when two successive groups of angels object to the creation. God—in the Jewish sources—does not ask the angels to worship Adam. On the contrary, He warns them against doing so. It is a moot point, whether سجد means here divine worship. In the Koran it is used of the homage paid to Joseph by his brethren. The story of the Talmud was also used in its original form, Tab. I, 86, 2, where angels are said to have objected to the creation of man and to have been burned. The objecting angels now appear as Jinn. Thus the talmudic story is used for the Christian theme of divine worship for Adam, as well as for the objection of the angels.

Tab. 1, 85: "And others say, Iblis was one of the remnant of the Jinn who were on earth, shed blood in it, did mischief in it, and rebelled against their master. And the angels fought them... The angels were fighting the Jinn, and Iblis was taken prisoner as a youth.[85] And he was with the angels. He worshipped Adam, then Iblis refused. And on this account God said: 'Iblis was one of the Jinn'." (Koran XVIII, 48).[86]

Tab. 1.85. "And it has been said that the cause of his destruction was the fact that the Jinn lived on earth before Adam, and God sent Iblis to judge among them and he ceased not judging rightly for a 1000 years so that he was called 'The Authority'[87] and God revealed to him His real name;[88] and through that he became proud and arrogant.

---

[85] According to the narrators mentioned above, Iblis had been sent to fight the rebellious Jinn, his victory over them puffed him up with pride, etc. Now here he is one of the rebellious Jinn, is taken prisoner and brought to heaven. Here the tendency of the tradition is most clear.

The Moslem shares the Jewish conception of Angels as beings who cannot sin. Iblis has sinned, consequently he cannot have been an angel. But he was in heaven. Nevertheless he must not be an angel. He becomes therefore a rebellious Jinn who improves in heavenly company, but shows his real nature when disobeying God's command to "worship" Adam.

According to this theory he was neither king nor 'treasurer'. Tabari I, 179, brings as evidence for the fact that Iblis was not an angel: (1) Iblis had offspring, whilst angels do not multiply; (2) he was created from fire whilst angels are created from light; (3) Iblis had passions(pride), angels are incapable of passion. All the same it remains true that from the text of the Koran no conclusive evidence is possible in either direction. The ﺨﻤﺼ may, but need not be applied. In all versions it is an angel (Lucifer, Satan) who sinned. Yet any book rightly demands to be read in the spirit and with the tradition of its own race. And ﺳﺠﺪ is inconclusive, for it is used for ordinary veneration of human beings in the Koran, 12 (Joseph's brethren).

[86] According to Jallal-ed-Din, Iblis begat the Jinn after his fall; he is 'Father of the Jinn'. Also Tab. I, 179 says, 'Iblis was the father of the Jinn, as Adam was the father of man'. Cp. Samael-Satan who with Eve begets Cain, the Father of Demons.

[87] This may perhaps be coupled with the version which makes man's creation the direct outcome of Iblis' rebellion. (As a judge Iblis appears also in the Zuhra legend.) The very same argument appears in Aelfric. It is not Jewish. And it is interesting to observe how the data of the creation of angels, genii, Satan, and man were fixed and combined to suit this story. See App. on 'Ersatztheorie'. There is no trace through all Jewish Literature (Kabbalah not excepted) of any idea that man was created as a substitute for a fallen angel or any group of fallen angels.

[88] The knowledge of God's real name bestows very great power. Zuhra elicits the Shem Hammephorash from the faithless judges, and by means of it she ascends to heaven. They also had judged for a long time in truth and equity. About the Shem Hammephorash, see Gruenbaum, *Neue Beiträge*, 2nd edition.

"And to this refers: 'Is our power exhausted by the first creation, etc.'" (Koran. 50, 14).[89]

Tab. 1.80. "Ibn Harig interprets Sura 21, 30: 'Whosoever shall say, I am a God beside man, that (angel) shall I reward with hell', to refer to Iblis: 'None said it but Iblis, who called for the worship of himself, and this verse came down respecting Iblis.'"

There are several questions to be answered before the origin of this incident can be determined. Firstly: What is the meaning of سجد in this place? (a) What *can* the meaning be? (b) What seems to be the force of it? (c) How do the commentators take it? Adam, according to Jewish lore, was not to be worshipped. The angels just prepare his food. In Christian accounts he, the prototype of Jesus, receives divine homage.[90] To determine the origin of the above verse we shall have to bring evidence that (a) سجد means merely the bow of politeness—then the source of this verse may have been Jewish; (b) it has the meaning of השתחויה in the Mishnah, the tribute due to a divinity; then the story is borrowed from Christian lore; (c) the meaning may elude exact definition, then the context may decide.

سجد occurs both for 'divine worship'[91] (the usual meaning), and for the polite bow due to a man of importance. Joseph's

[89] The citation (Koran L. 14) is here used illustratively rather than logically. The passage is believed to refer to the resurrection. I believe the narrator had the first part in mind, viz: 'Is our power exhausted by the first creation? No! We shall create man in place of fallen Iblis and his troop.'

[90] 1 Corinth. 15.45. "And so it is written: 'The first man, Adam, was made a living soul; the last Adam a quickening spirit'." This view is the psychological basis for the great honor (the worship by angels) accorded to Adam in Christian writings. Jewish lore had no such tendency, hence there is only a counter tendency visible, reducing the glorious Adam to a mere mortal.

[91] Tab. 8, *ad locum* (see also Jallal-ed-Din), who has most reliable traditions, considers سجد as referring not to divine worship, but to civil homage. The Mohammedans —to whom Jesus is not a god—would naturally reflect the divinity of Adam; but the atter's claim to such honors is only based on the supposition that he is the prototype of Jesus. Thus Mohammed took this story over, unconscious of its meaning, and it was left to his commentators to right the matter by making (a) Iblis a Jinn, (b) سجد a civil homage.

brethren (Sura XLI, 161) bow to him, and it cannot be claimed that they mean to prostrate themselves before him as before a divine being; also in the Muallaḳāt سجد occurs in the same sense. Thus the decision rests not with سجد in the Koran but with the question of what سجد *must* mean *here*. The answer will depend upon the attitude of the Koran towards the deification of Adam. If another instance be found, the Christian origin of this story may be considered probable. If not, we have no reason for regarding it as such. The opposite is the case. Not even Mohammed is deified before the advent of Neo-platonic syncretism.[92]

With the meaning of سجد undetermined; with the fact that the angels desired to call Adam 'Holy' (Genesis Rabba) showing that even in Jewish sources there was the sense of Adam's greatness; with the total absence from any portion of the Koran of any attempt at deification; with the سجد in Sura, 12, in any case, it is possible to decide one way or the other. That Iblis occurs in all the passages would only then be a, minor, proof of its Christian origin if it occurred in no other connection, in no story which is taken from evidently Jewish sources. But it does occur in such stories (cp. Sura 7), where Iblis becomes Satan in the source of one chapter, thus being identified with the latter. Mohammed heard the name and combined it with his story.[93]

Jallal-al-Din takes سجد to mean here civil worship or homage paid to creatures.

---

[92] In spite of all this it appears to me that Iblis (سجد) is Christian. Iblis does occur in all these passages and in no other. Tab. is the later tendency. Pugio Fidei is late. But see Gruenbaum on Shaytan, p. 291.

[93] Tab. 180. Ibn Harig in the course of interpreting Koran XXI, 30 says that it refers to Iblis, the enemy of God. On Geiger's suggestion this would be additional proof that even the misinterpretation of Isaiah 13 came to Islam through Christian sources.

The Account in Pugio Fidei

Pugio Fidei 563: Satan falls "because he refuses to worship Adam."

R. Joshua ben Nun:[94] "When the mind of Adam matured in him[95] the Holy One blessed be He, said to the ministering angels, 'Worship ye him!' They came (and did so) in accordance with his wishes. And Satan was greater than all the angels of heaven.[96] And he said to God: 'Lord of the Universe! Thou hast created us from the splendor of the Shekinah and Thou sayest that we should bow down before him whom Thou hast created from the dust of the ground?' The Holy One blessed be He answered: 'He who is made from the dust of the earth has wisdom and understanding which thou dost not possess'.[97] And it came to pass, when he would not worship him, nor hearken to the voice of God, that He cast him out of heaven and he became Satan. To him refers Isaiah's 'How art thou fallen, etc.'"

This is the only 'Jewish' story of God commanding Satan to worship Adam. It is also the only story in the whole range of rabbinic literature of an angel, even Satan, refusing to obey the command of the Lord. Angels, it is true, are punished, but either because they made a mistake or because they were indiscreet. (See App. 'Other fallen angels'.)

There is no indication whatever anywhere of angels being rebellious. This consideration alone would suffice to throw much doubt on the authenticity as a Jewish story of this extract from the Midrash of Rabbi Moses ha-Darshan. But the MS. of this Midrash is at hand, and in it the second part of the story in *Pugio* is absent. In

---
[94] See Epstein, *Eldad had-Dani*, p. 42.
[95] See philological note below.
[96] This is not to be found in any Jewish source.
[97] The following three lines are not in the Prague MS.; this is very significant.

the MS. Satan asks for the reason of God's command, receives the answer, and there the matter rests. Now Rabbi Moses lived at Narbonne at the time when the Koran was well known in Spain. God's command to worship Adam, as related in the Koran, might have induced him to introduce it into his Midrash; omitting, however, the motive of Satan's refusal.

A later hand, seeing the MS., added from his own knowledge the latter part. Thus we might account for the discrepancy between *Pugio* and the MS.—Geiger, however, remains right as against Zunz (*Gottesd. Vorträge*, 291) in considering the story of God's command that the angels should worship Adam as essentially Christian. As to the reliability of *Pugio*, see Neubauer, *Tobit*, also *Expositor*, I, 9, and Epstein, in *Magazin*, 1888. Epstein shows that the Prague MS. lacks the part beginning 'and it came to pass', the MS. ending with 'which thou dost not possess.' Epstein mentions Hillel ben Samuel (13th cent.), who says in his book תגמולי הנפש: "It is written in some homiletical books that one group of angels fell from heaven at the beginning of the creation of the world; and these scholars rely for their view on some misunderstood verses, e. g. 'How art thou fallen from heaven, etc.'" Both Steinschneider and Epstein think that Hillel by 'some homiletical books' refers to Rabba Rabbeti. I am not quite convinced of it because Hillel speaks of a group of angels, while the R. R. refers to one angel only. The angels of Genesis 6.1–4 are neither a group nor yet does their fall take place 'in the beginning of the creation of the world.'

However that may be, Hillel represents the Jewish tradition in his rejection of any story about disobedient angels. He forms a link, over more than a thousand years, with Simon bar Yohai.

Hillel is very indignant in his expressions: "I consider

this an empty silly belief, devoid of any foundation."

To any one familiar with rabbinic texts the Hebrew of this passage appears very peculiar.

(1) Grünbaum has already drawn attention to the fact that דבר is used for 'said' instead of אמר, which is quite unusual. "The whole mode of expression is somewhat raw."

(2) ביום שנתקבצה אליו דעתו של אדם is very odd—'On the day when the mind of Adam was gathered to him.'

(3) Arabisms: (a) לאשר יצרת אותו (b) יש בו מן החכמה.

The fact that "Die Darstellung in Gen. Rabba eine auffallende Ähnlichkeit mit der im Koran hat", is not to be taken, as Grünbaum does, as a proof that Mohammed used a Jewish story, but that the story of the *Pugio*—whether a genuine or a spurious Midrash—is taken from the Koran either directly or indirectly. For this speaks especially the fact that in no Jewish source is Satan "the greatest of the angels"; as Samael, he is head of the Shedim, who have nothing to look for in heaven, but among the angels he by no means occupies, nor did he ever occupy, any very prominent position.

The reasons against taking the *Pugio Fidei* account for genuine Jewish lore are: (1) Argumentum e silentio of the story, (2) Argumentum e silentio of Satan's greatness, (3) The odd Hebrew of the passage, (4) The fact that the stories about Adam reveal rather the opposite tendency, that of insisting on his mere humanity, (5) The fact that the Prague MS. omits the fall of Satan. But the reasons for assuming this to be taken from the Koran are: (1) Similarity of main features and of words; (2) نار v. זו – طين v. עפר v. השתחוו לו אסجدوا لآدم as Grünbaum has already noticed. (3) R. Moses lived near a Moslem uncotry, knew Arabic and without doubt also the Koran.

Epstein has proved that R. Rabbeti is a compilation which seems to have gone through various editions. It appears to have contained material either non-Jewish or against the spirit of the Midrash. The Prague MS. differs in language from *Pugio* in several details; it omits any mention of Satan's rebellion. We have thus one part of a text, borrowed in the 11th century, which speaks of a command to worship Adam. And the other half, though reminiscent of the Koran, speaks of Satan's fall based on Isaiah 14. R. Moses' work "Yesod" contains extracts from older Midrashim and Midrashic elements 'of his own making'. See Bacher (in Winter und Wünsche, II, 270, 335); Epstein, R. Moses Hadarshan, 1891.

Chapter 5.

THE FALL OF MAN

(A) The Serpent Before the Fall

The Serpent had two horns,[98] (stood upright) and had two feet. Gen. R. 19.

The jealousy of the Serpent is proved from the text. Gen. 2.25 should be followed by 3.21; the story of the Serpent is interpolated to give the reason for his action. He saw Adam and Eve, in blissful ignorance of shame, happy in their love, and he became jealous and envious.

(Gen. R. 18). Another cause of the Serpent's jealousy. R. Judah b. Bathyra[99] said: "Adam was sitting in the Garden of Eden and the ministering angels were roasting meat for him and giving him clear wine. The Serpent came, saw his honor and envied him."

---

[98] Fleischer, in Levy's Dictionary I, 442, Bacher 1, 10, 2 agreeing: דיקרטים= neither δίκροτος, "zweirudrig", here "zweiflüssig", nor δίκορσος, "zweiköpfig", but דיקרסטים=δικεράστης,"having two horns", composed of δίς and κεράστης. Mussafia, however, connects the word with Latin "directus". That would give good sense. In the Ms. mentioned by Perles (*Zur rabbin. Sprachkunde*, 12) it reads קופֿן=upright, instead of דיקרטים, which evidently is intended as a translation of the former.

[99] Of the second generation of the Tannaim (90–130 C.E.). Tanna is a teacher who is mentioned in the Mishnah or who lived at that time.

In the Midrash, the Serpent, a fully developed, beautiful animal, walking upright, causes man to fall because he would like him to be put to death as a punishment for eating of the forbidden fruit. The main purpose, however, of the Serpent is not the death of Adam, but the possession of his widow Eve. Because he saw their joys of love, he lusted after Eve.

Rabbi[100] said: "Had the Serpent not been cursed, he would have been a great benefit to man, to be used instead of horse, mule, ass. Every man would possess two serpents, sending the one northward, the other southward for thirty days. They would bring him silver, gold, jewels and pearls."

(B) The Serpent and Eve

Babli Sotah 9b. "Whosoever aspires to what does not belong to him, not only does not receive what he asks, but that which he has is taken from him. Thus do we find it with the ancient serpent, who aspired to what was not suitable for him, (with the result that) what he asked was not given to him and what he had possessed was taken from him."

The Holy One blessed be He said: "I had intended to make thee king over all cattle and beasts, now 'thou art cursed from all cattle and from all the beasts of the field'[101] (Gen. 3, 14). I had intended to let him walk upright, now 'on his belly shall he go'.[102] I had intended human food to be his food, now 'dust shall he eat'".

[100] Rabbi Judah I, ha-Nassi, the Prince, the Patriarch (see Strack, *Einleitung in Talmud und Midrasch*, p. 133), compiled the Mishnah; he is called "the Holy" because of his severely moral life.

[101] This indicates that the serpent (though "one of the beasts of the field" and not identified with a spirit of evil) must have been originally different in appearance and mode of progression. Its crawling on the ground is regarded as the fulfilment of the curse pronounced in the garden.

[102] In this light the Sefer Ḥasidim which speaks of the Serpent as a man, walking upright, can be understood rightly. And all the stories speaking of his "adultery" with Eve (cp. Rashi) have some foundation. Cf. Wisdom II, 24, Rev. XX, 2 for the later development of the story.

"He had said: 'I shall slay Adam and marry Eve', and now enmity shall I put between thee and the woman and between thy seed and her seed".[103]

Targ. Jon. *ad loc.*: "The serpent began to speak slander against his Creator and said to the woman: 'You shall surely not die, etc.'"

Gen. R. 19.4: Rabbi Joshua of Siknin in the name of R. Levi:[104] "He (the serpent) began to say slanderous things[105] against his Creator, saying, 'He ate from this tree and thus was able to create the world, and He forbade you to eat from it lest you create other worlds.'"

(C) The Punishment of the Serpent

Pirke de R. E. 20, Targ. Jon. *ad loc.*: "From the skin of the serpent.[106] God made unto Adam and Eve skin coats of honor, as it is said, 'And God made to Adam and his wife coats of skin'.

And He cut off the feet of the serpent and decreed that it should cast its skin and suffer pain once in seven years, and cursed it that it should drag itself with its belly on the ground, and its food is turned in its belly into dust[107] and gall of asps and death is in its mouth;[108] and He put

---

[103] Cp. Ryle, Genesis 54. "The hostility between the Serpent and the woman, between the Serpent's seed and the woman's seed, typifies the unending conflict between all that represents the forces of evil on the one hand, and all that represents the true and high destiny of mankind on the other." When later, after Demons and Satans and their kinsfolk peopled the air, the identification of the serpent with Satan had taken place, it was accomplished as the result of some dim consciousness that the enmity between woman and serpent meant more than the mere "instinctive antipathy of mankind toward the serpent". The only difference between the earlier and the later period, hac in re, lies in the fact that in earlier times there was no conception of a "personal enemy", of Satan as mankind's foe, so that the character (the deeper one) of the serpent remained abstract in the consciousness of those who knew the Law, until, with the influx of Babylonian (Persian) lore, Satan became a concrete entity and the Serpent its Bible representative.

[104] Second Century C. E.

[105] דילטוריה *delatura*.

[106] The Serpent apparently cast its skin at once, at the commencement of the seven years, and the material was used for the coats of honor. The two passages thus explain each other.

[107] Targ-Pseudo-Jon.: *ad loc.*: "Thou shalt be cursed from all the cattle and the beasts of the field, on thy belly shalt thou go and thy feet shall be cut off and thy skin will be cast every seven years and deadly venom shall be in thy mouth, and thou shalt eat dust all the days of thy life."

[108] Cp. the Homilies of Isaac of Antioch, ed. Bedjan, p. 12.

hatred between it and the children of the woman so that they should bruise its head, and after all these (curses cometh) death."

Cp. Schatzhöhle p. 9: "The Serpent's feet I have withdrawn into his body and I have given him the dust of the earth as his food."

Gen. R. 19; "When the Holy One blessed be He, said to the Serpent; 'Thou shalt walk upon thy belly', the ministering angels descended and cut off his hands and his feet, and the voice of his cries went from one end of the world to the other end.

"And the Lord God brought the three of them to judgment, and He said to the Serpent: 'Because thou hast done this, thou art cursed from all cattle and the beasts of the field; on thy belly shalt thou walk and thy feet shall be cut off and thy slough shall be cast once in seven years and a deadly venom shall be in thy mouth and thou shalt eat dust all the days of thy life. And enmity shall I put between thee and between the woman, between thy posterity and her posterity. And it shall be, when the children of the woman shall be keeping the laws of the Torah, they shall aim[109] and smite thee on thy head, and when they shall be forsaking the laws of the Torah, thou shalt aim and bruise their heels. But they shall have healing[110] and thou shalt have no healing. And they shall make peace with each other in the last days of the Messiah (Cp. Targ. Jon. *ad loc.*).'"[111]

---

[109] מכוונין either "aiming or smiting": for the former cp. Gen. 49.14,f. Numb. 34.7; for the latter Prov. 23.35.

[110] Cp. Gen. Rabb. *ad loc.*: "All shall have healing except the serpent". The above passage has some eschatological ring about it. Cp. it with the destruction (in the N.T.) of the Kingdom of Satan who also will have no peace. As to Origen's view that Satan will be finally redeemed see *sub* Harut.

[111] Schuerer and Charles would call this Midrash a "pharisaical exploitation". It is only an essay in exegetics. The Serpent, in any case, is a type already of the future Satan, for it can do harm only where the law of God is not kept. But Pseudo-Jonathan has many interpolations of the 7th and 8th centuries c. E., so that the presence here of these notions is no evidence of their early incorporation in Jewish folklore.

Gen. R., 20, 4: "Thou art cursed." Rabbi Joshua of Siknin in the name of R. Levi said: "He cursed him with leprosy. Those scales of the serpent are (marks of) leprosy."

R. Eleazar thinks it is due to the curse that "the serpent brings forth only once in seven years".

Revelation of Moses: "Cursed art thou of all the beasts. Upon thy breast and belly shalt thou go and thou shalt be deprived both of thy hands and feet; there shall not be granted thee ear, nor wing, nor one limb."

(D) PUNISHMENT OF ADAM AND EVE.

The Fall of Man [112]

Abot de R. Nathan, I, ed. Schechter, p. 4:[112a] "God had commanded Adam saying, 'Of every tree of the garden thou mayest freely eat. But of the tree of knowledge of good and evil thou shalt not eat of it; for in the day that thou eatest thereof, thou shalt surely die'. Adam did not wish to tell it to Eve, as the Holy One blessed be He had told her himself.[113] But he said (to Eve): 'But of the fruit of the tree which is in the middle of the garden, God said, Ye shall not eat of it, neither shall ye touch it,[114] lest ye die'.

"At that time the wicked Serpent considered in his heart

---

[112] For the Consequence of the Fall of Man see also Appendix II.

[112a] Whereas some parts of this book are undoubtedly the work of R. Nathan, the greater part was collected and edited after the completion of the Talmud (6th cent.). R. Nathan lived in the 2nd century (in the 4th generation of Tannaim).

[113] This is a commentary on the saying "Make a fence round the Law," i. e. guard it against transgression by forbidding things allowed which might lead to a transgression of the law in question. Examples are given of God, the Torah, Moses, etc., acting in this manner. Adam too made a fence round the command of God, by saying the divine prohibition included also the touching of the tree. In another place the evil consequences of his deed are held up as a warning to those who wish to add to the laws of God by prohibiting to themselves things allowed.

[114] There is no evidence in the text that Adam told Eve, "Neither shall ye touch it", but as Eve could have heard it only from Adam, the Commentator draws the inference that she reported Adam correctly. See version "B".

and said: 'Since I am unable to cause Adam to fall,[115] I shall go and cause Eve to fall'. He went, sat beside her, and talked much with her. He told her: 'If thou meanest that God commanded us concerning the touching of the tree, behold I touch it and yet I am not dead'. What did the wicked Serpent do now? He stood up and touched the tree with his hands and his feet, and shook it (so violently) that its fruits fell to the ground...

"And again he said: 'If thou mean that God's command refers to eating the fruit (i. e. that eating it would cause your death), lo, I am eating of it[116] and yet I am not dead, neither shalt thou die from eating it.'

"Eve thought: 'All the things commanded by my Lord[117] are futile.'[118] She took it and ate at once and gave to Adam (afterwards) and he ate it...

"Who caused this 'touching'?[119] The 'fence' which Adam had made about his words. Hence our Sages say, 'A man who makes a fence about his words (promises, plans) will be unable to carry them through'. Hence they also said, 'Let none add anything to what he has heard!'[120]

"What did the wicked Serpent plan at that moment? 'I shall go and slay Adam[121] and marry his wife, and I

[115] Adam's caution in making the fence discouraged the Serpent. Here is no trace of either envy or jealousy on the part of the Serpent. Apparently we have the oldest text, free from foreign embellishments.

[116] That is an incident unrecorded elsewhere. Nor does it appear necessary for the argument here. Also the other view, i. e. that to add to the Commandments of God is wrong, could dispense with the Serpent's eating the fruit. By remaining alive after having touched it, he had established his case and proved that the transgression of the commandment did not cause death. There was no difference in Eve's mind between touching and eating.

[117] For Eve, at first, called her husband only "My lord".

[118] Lit: "All the things (words)...are false (a lie).

[119] With its disastrous consequences.

[120] There is an inconsistency between the head and the tail of the argument. The text reads: "And make a fence about the Law"; the Commentator adds: "As Adam made one about his words". One would expect that the following narrative would show the benefit accruing from the fence. But the result is a warning not to make a fence about one's words. Shall we assume that "fence" by association of ideas brought the story of Adam before the writer's mind and that he wrote it down unconscious of its ending? Or does he mean that we ought to make a fence but with all discretion?

[121] I. e. cause him to die by transgressing the command of God. But then he apparently forgot his scheme, for he "killed" Eve whom he desired to possess.

shall be king over all the world and shall go about proudly,[122] and shall enjoy royal pleasures (luxuries).'

"And whence do we know that Adam made a fence about his words? God had told him: 'Of every tree of the garden thou mayest eat, but of the tree of knowledge thou must not eat'. From the words of Eve, however, we learn that he had made a fence (in forbidding her to touch it). The serpent debated the matter with himself and said: 'If I were to go to Adam, I know he would not hearken unto me; I will go to Eve, for women—as I know—listen to (obey) every man'. Thereupon he went and said, etc.

"She answered: '...but from the fruit of the tree in the midst of the garden God said, You shall not eat thereof, nor shall ye touch it, lest ye die'.

"When the Serpent heard this, he found a door to enter by, i. e. to succeed in persuading her to eat."

Consequences of the Fall of Man

Ibidem. With ten curses Eve was cursed at that time. As it is said: 'I shall greatly (1) multiply (2) thy sorrow (3) and thy conception, (4) in sorrow (5) shalt thou bring forth (6) children, (7) and thy desire (8) shall be to thy husband, (9) and he shall rule (10) over thee.' What caused all this? The fence of Adam.

R. Judah b. Bathyra said: "On that day three decrees were decreed against Adam, as it is said, 'And to Adam He said: Because thou hast hearkened unto the voice of thy wife and hast eaten of the tree, (1) Cursed is the ground for thy sake. (2) In toil shalt thou eat of it all the days of thy life. (3) Thorns also and thistles shall it bring forth unto thee, and thou shalt eat the herb

---

[122] Since the Serpent is conceived as walking upright, קומה זקופה here is to be taken figuratively. In this sense it occurs in rabbinic laws: "Go not about בקומה זקופה, arrogantly".

of the field.' When Adam heard that the Holy One blessed be He told him 'And thou shalt eat the herb of the field', his limbs trembled. He said before Him: 'Lord of the Universe! Shall I and my cattle eat in one crib?' The Holy One blessed be He replied: 'Considering that thy limbs trembled (at the thought), thou shalt eat bread in the sweat of thy brow'.[123]

"And three decrees were equally decreed against Eve:
'(1) I shall greatly multiply thy sorrow and thy conception.
(2) In sorrow shalt thou bring forth children.
(3) Thy desire shall be to thy husband and he shall rule over thee.'

"When the day grew near eventide, Adam saw the world getting dark and, turning westwards, he said, 'Woe unto me, because I have rebelled; the Lord, on my account, is plunging the whole world into darkness!' He knew not that this (evening) was the natural course.

"At morn, when he saw the world full of light, he came eastwards and was exceedingly glad; he built altars, brought an ox whose horns had grown before its hoofs and offered it up as a burnt-offering, as it is said: 'And it shall please the Lord better than an ox or a bullock that hath horns and hoofs' (Ps. 69.32).

"In that hour three groups of ministering angels came down and in their hands were harps and flutes and musical instruments of all sorts and they sang with him a song, as it is said: 'A Psalm, being a song, for the Sabbath day'". (According to the Midrash this psalm was composed by Adam.)

"'Cursed is the ground for thy sake', i. e. it will bring up for thee cursed things—wasps, fleas and flies."

When the Serpent was with Eve he infected her with

---

[123] "When Adam heard that he would have to work in the sweat of his brow, he became calm again."

lasciviousness.[124] Rashi, *ad locum*, points הִשִּׂיאַנִי, i. e. while persuading me to eat of the fruit, he "married" me, made me his wife. To the misplacement of the dot this story may be due. But is seems more likely that the dot was misplaced ad hoc, so as to find a hint in the text for it.

These accounts in my mind appear to fit the sense of the original. They are faithful to the text or introduce nothing foreign to the spirit of Genesis 3. The Serpent, a healthy, exceptionally clever beast, becomes envious of Adam's marital happiness, or of his honor among the angels, or of his rule over all beasts, or he becomes enamoured of Eve and desires to win her by all means. For that reason he seems to have intended originally to persuade Adam to eat of the fruit of the tree. The consequent death of Adam would make Eve free for himself. He abandons his original plan, either because he finds on second thought that Adam would successfully resist his temptation, or because, coming near Eve, he forgets all about his plans. He persuades her, brings upon her the curses set forth in Genesis, brings curses upon Adam as described there, and himself is reduced from an upright beast into a crawling reptile. According to another version, he goes in unto Eve and infests her with lasciviousness. It appears, however, that this latter point is taken from the Samael-cycle.

Man, contrite and truly repentant, seems to regain the divine favor, for the angels come down and sing in chorus the 92nd Psalm, "composed on the first Sabbath of the world by the first man of the world".

It is a story of sin, punishment, repentance. Beyond death, the pains of child-bearing and the sweat of the brow no sign appears of any lasting damnation.

---

[124] Being a beast, in spite of all his superiority to his fellow beasts, he left some beastliness in Eve, in the form of lasciviousness (הטיל בה זוהמא).

So far the original undiluted Jewish accounts of the Fall of Man caused by the Serpent.

In Abot V there is an interesting document of an early conception of natural law. The exceptions to natural law—the miracles—are represented as having been created before the world was quite complete, i. e. together with the rule. And it is valuable to note that an important "miracle" has been omitted. But let the text speak for itself.

Ten things were created between the suns:[125] The mouth of the Earth and the mouth of the well (see Rashi on Num. 21.17) and the mouth of the ass (of Balaam) and the rainbow (Gen. 9.13) and the manna and the rod (see Pirke de R. E. 40) and the *shamir* worm (see sub Ashmedai) and the shape of the written characters and the writing and the tables.

Yet the speech of the serpent—in the minds of the Sages—was not a miracle, or it too would have been mentioned in connection with the mouth of the ass.

This again shows that the Serpent was considered as a being gifted with speech.

(E) Samael's Part in the Fall of Man

Samael and the Serpent are frequently identified in this connection, as is evident from a perusal of the last chapter, yet may it not be superfluous to compare the texts which speak of Samael only.

(1) Samael and the Serpent

Targum J. Genesis 3.6: "And the woman saw Samael the Angel of Death and she grew afraid."

She saw Samael in the serpent, after the serpent had spoken his slander; not before. This is at once text and

---

[125] בין השמשות "twilight". For an interesting parallel see M. Sidersky in *Journal of the Royal Asiatic Society*, 1921, No. 1.

commentary. She saw him at the moment she was about to sin.

Yalkut Gen.25: "Samael took his band with him and chose for himself the cunning and malicious serpent, mounted him and rode upon him down to earth."

A comparison of these texts shows at once the late date of the Yalkut; the Targum, like all the older Midrashim, knows nothing of Samael's band. (Cp. Lucifer's band). The Yalkut was compiled in the 13th century. See Zunz, *Gottesdienstliche Vorträge*, 2nd edition, p. 311f.

(2) Samael and Eve.

Targum J. Genesis 4.1: "And Adam knew Eve his wife, who was pregnant by the angel Samael, and she conceived and bore Cain; and he was like heavenly beings, and not like earthly beings, and she said, 'I have acquired a man with the angel of the Lord.'"

Pirke de R. E., 21: "Samael riding on the Serpent came to her and she conceived; afterwards Adam came to her and she conceived Abel, as it is said, 'And Adam knew his wife' (Genesis 4.1). What is the meaning of 'knew'? He knew that she had conceived. And she saw his likeness that it was not of the earthly beings, but of the heavenly beings, and she prophesied and said: 'I have gotten a man with the Lord'."

Zohar, Gen. 4.1: "Samael came in unto Eve, infected her with lasciviousness (lit: filth), and she became pregnant and bore Cain. And his face was not like that of other human beings, and all those who descend from him are called 'Bene Elohim'."[126]

Yalkut Hadash *ad. loc.*: "This evil in Cain[127] caused him to kill Abel."

---

[126] The rational tradition in the Zohar.
[127] The effect of זוהמא which destroys alike soul and body.

Ibid 1,52: "Samael begot the spirit, the soul of Cain, Adam became his bodily father. The Samael-created spirit had no body until Adam's seed supplied it."

(3) Identifications of Samael with Satan and the Serpent

Exodus Rabba 18, 1: "To whom are Michael and Samael to be compared? To the advocate and prosecutor, who stand before the court. Thus Michael and Samael stand before God; Samael accuses and Michael defends Israel."

Yalkut Hadash 78: "Samael is identical with the serpent and with Satan."

This is an apparently new function of Satan. As angel of death he suffers neither loss of, nor addition to, his original attributes; he killed by God's command the firstborn of Egypt and he slays by the same authority all who are to die. Neither is the Yezer Hara' (Evil Inclination) anything previously unknown, for Satan tempts David to do evil. It is only in his identification with the Serpent that the new lore has invaded the haggadic fields.

See also Gen. Rabba 56, where Samael endeavors to tempt both Abraham and Isaac; and Deut. R. 11, where Samael as the Angel of Death comes for the soul of Moses.

Schatzhöhle, III (Eve tells of Satan's crafty deception): "And he put upon the fruit which he gave me to eat the poison of his wickedness, that is, of his desire, for desire is the head (another version: has root and origin) of all sin.

"God grudges her and Adam the knowledge of good and evil, this is the reason of his prohibition to eat. The Devil (speaking through the mouth of the serpent) causes her to swear by the throne of God, the Cherubim, and the Tree of Life that she will give Adam of the forbidden fruit."

The Serpent himself is beguiled by Satan. It must be so, for Satan, 'fighting God', is the power of evil.

(4) Etymology of Samael

Babli Abodah Zarah 20b: "People tell of the angel of death that when a sick man dies, he stands above the head of his bed, his sword drawn in his hand and a drop of gall suspended therefrom. When the sick man sees him he trembles and opens his mouth, and Samael pours it into his mouth.'

Samael = poison of God, which ends man's life.

Chapter 6

ASHMEDAI

(A) Ashmedai and Aeshma

Ashmedai may be Aeshma etymologically; he is by no means Aeshma as far as his character or his functions are concerned.

As Grünbaum rightly remarks, Kohut's efforts to identify the natures of these two spirits must fail. Carried away by his etymological 'evidence', Kohut appears to overlook all passages which clearly demonstrate his theory to be untenable; his usual acumen also fails him in the interpretation of the passages he does cite.
"Aeshma is the main helper of Angromainyus."
"He commands an army of demons."
"Aeshma helps Angromainyus against Ahura Mazda."
"Aeshma is the ancestor of all Daevas which Angromainyus has brought forth to destroy all purity in the world."
"Aeshma is the personification of physical dissolution."
"All knowledge and science comes from Aeshma."
"He is one of the demons aiming at the overthrow of the moral order of the world."

All these citations are from Kohut. I shall now present the features of Ashmedai in rabbinic literature, to make clear the differences between him and Aeshma.

Talmud B. Pesaḥim 110a: "Ashmedai is the king of all Shedim and as king is not a harmful spirit".

Giṭṭin 68a: "Ashmedai allows himself to be carried away as soon as he hears that "The Name of thy Lord is upon thee". "He goes out of his way to spare the widow's hut." "He saves a wicked drunkard to cause him to enjoy his life." "He weeps at the early death of the merrymaking bridegroom, and at the hope deferred of his widow to be." "He is as sensual as a he-goat, whose feet he has." "He has come by the command of God to take Solomon's throne in order to punish his disobedience and offending self-reliance." Note also MS. Munich and the fact that according to other versions an angel, not Ashmedai, came down to punish Solomon.

Evidently Ashmedai has nothing but the name in common with the Parsee demon.[128]

In the first part of the Talmudical story he is a jolly, good-natured spirit, fond of drink, in the second part the predominant feature is the punishment of Solomon. So that quite apart from the divergence in details, the two principal differences become emphatic: (1) Aeshma is essentially malevolent, the enemy of man, who is the creature of Ahura Mazda. Ashmedai is a good-natured being; he is the servant of God, and though loose in his morals he is absolutely obedient to Him (see below). (2) Aeshma endeavors to destroy man by the command and in pursuit of the aim of Angromainyus. Ashmedai comes to punish Solomon by the command of God. He is prince of the Sheddim, *not* a harmful spirit.

I am adding a complete translation of the passage in Giṭṭin 68a, so that my claims may be judged from the text itself.

---

[128] But see Whitehouse in Hastings' *Dictionary of the Bible*, who contends that not even the name is connected with Aeshma, but with השמיד = שמד.

(B) The Ashmedai Text in Babli Gittin 68a

Ecclesiastes 2.8: "I provided me male and female musicians[129] and the luxuries of the sons of men."

These two words we translate here (in Babylonia) by 'demons and demonesses'; in the west (in Palestine) they say it means 'a chair' (or a 'chest') (a chariot or sedan chair for the use of women and princes, Rashi). Rabbi Joḥanan said: 'There were three hundred demons (or chests, see Jastrow *s. v.*) at Sihin, but what "shida" in itself means, I do not know'. (It appears more likely that R. Joḥanan hesitated to express an opinion on Shedim, except to say that he did not know what the nature of a box is. He is evidently referring to some popular story according to which three hundred spirits are haunting the "unfortunate" city. And being asked what he thought about it, he quieted or dismissed the questioner in the bove manner).[130]

---

[129] The main interpretations of these ambiguous words are (1) LXX οἰνοχόον καὶ οἰνοχόας, male and female cup-bearers; this may be strengthened by referring to שׁדא, Syr., שׁדא which in the Talmud often means "to pour"; it has a similar though not the identical meaning in Syriac; see Payne-Smith, *Thesaurus* 4063. Aquila's κυλίκιον may perhaps be due to a different application of the same idea. It is evident that the Targum: "tubes which pour forth tepid and hot water respectively" מרובין דשדין takes שׁדא to be the root. Barton's "*cold* water" is a mistake.

(2) Root Ar. شدّ denoting intensity, strength, thus "multitude of all things", "a heap and heaps".

(3) ستر to hide—thus "woman of the harem".

(4) سند to lean upon—thus "bed" and "concubine".

(5) The Talmud derives it from Ass. sidu "bull deity"; in Arabic سيّد "Lord". The Palestinian "chair" may be due to سند. It means "chest" however also in Babylonia. Ket. 65a acc. to Jastrow *s. v.*, also in Giṭṭin, *l. c.*

(6) שד breast—"female".

[130] According to Rashi: Some say that "Sheda" is the head of all of them, but I know nothing as to her nature or figure. The ordinary interpretation "what a Sheda is" seems preferable, esp. since a few lines below it is said that Ashmedai is the head (King) of the Shedim. But "Queen Lilith", an evil spirit, appears in Targum to Job 1.15, and those who take "Sheda" to be the queen may well have thought of her.

"It has been said: Here we translate by 'male and female demons'. What did Solomon need[131] them for? In I Kings 6.7 it is said: 'And the house when it was in building, was built of stone made ready at the quarry; and there was neither hammer nor axe nor any tool of iron heard in the house while it was in building'. Solomon asked the Rabbis, 'How can I do it (break the stones for the temple without iron tools)?[132] They told him: 'There is a stone for the purpose called "Shamir" which Moses brought for the stones of the Ephod'. 'Where is it to be found?' Solomon asked. They answered: "Cause demons and demonesses to come to thee, retain (or 'force', 'subdue') them together, it is possible that they know it and they may reveal it to you'.[133] He brought demons and demonesses, and forced them (to obey him) together: but they said, 'We do not know it. Perhaps Ashmedai, the king of the demons, knows it.' Solomon: 'Where is he?' The demons: 'He is on that and that mountain, has dug there a pit, filled it with water, covered it with a rock and sealed it with his ring. And every morning he ascends to heaven, learns the topics of the heavens, descends to the ground (earth) and learns the topics of the earth, he comes (down), inspects the seal, opens the pit, drinks the water, covers and seals the pit and goes off.' Solomon sent Benaiah,[133a] the son of Jehoiada, and gave him a chain on which the Name of God was engraved and a ring upon which the Name of God was engraved, bundles of wool and bottles of wine (filled with wine). He went and dug from below the pit, caused the water to come out slowly, and closed the hole with the bundles of wool. Then

[131] Lit: "him", the teller of the story thinks of Ashmedai, the main hero.

[132] Cp. Mishna Middot III, 4, Sotah 48b. "Iron was made to shorten the life of man; the altar was made to prolong the life of man, and it is not meet that that which shortens the life of man be lifted up above what prolongs it."

[133] It is an essential point for all comparisons between "shedim" and demons, that the former are not always malevolent, cp. Shabbat 67a. The demons help Solomon to build the temple. Giṭṭin 69b.

[133a] About Benaiah see also T. Babli Berakot 4a.

he dug a pit above the pit of Ashmedai, pouring the wine into it. He came (ascended) and sat on a tree. When Ashmedai came he examined the seal, broke it and found the wine. He said (to himself): 'Wine is a mocker, mead is a brawler; whoever is overtaken thereby, is not wise' (Prov. 20.1), and (he also meditated on how) 'Harlotry, wine and new wine take away the brain" (Hosea 4.2), and (as the result of this reflection) he did not drink it, at first. When he became thirsty, he could not withstand the temptation, he drank, became intoxicated and fell down (asleep). Benaiah descended from the tree and threw upon him the chain which he sealed (closed) with the ring. Ashmedai, on awaking, made efforts to get free, but Benaiah told him: 'The Name of thy Lord is upon thee, the Name of thy Lord is upon thee'. (Whereupon he allowed himself to be led away). He took hold of him and went. As Ashmedai came to a tree[134] he scratched himself against it and uprooted it, coming towards a house he overthrew it, when he reached the hut of a widow she came forth and asked him to be gracious (made supplication to him). He bent his body away from the house (so suddenly or violently that) a bone in him was broken, whereupon he said, 'This is the meaning of "Gentle words break the bone"'. He saw a blind man who strayed from his way and he brought him back to his way. He saw also a drunkard who strayed from his way and he brought him back to it. He saw a happy wedding party where people enjoyed themselves and he wept. He heard a man saying to a bootmaker, 'Make me shoes for seven

---

[134] Gruenbaum is at variance with Kohut as to what causes Ashmedai to uproot the tree. Kohut, with Aeshma constantly before his eyes, considers it due to Ashmedai's demoniacal passion for destruction. Gruenbaum thinks that Ashmedai's enormous bulk caused it. This view is the more plausible one, as there is no trace in the whole account of the demon's ill-will towards man or other creatures, as we have a direct statement (in the case of the widow) of his twisting his body so as to save the widow's home from being overthrown. This gives sense only if we assume Ashmedai to be very broad and tall. Also the statement that when freed from the chain, he rested one wing on earth, the other extending to heaven, intimates something of this sort

years', and he laughed. He saw a sorcerer practising witchcraft, and he laughed.[135] When he arrived at the palace, he was not brought before the King until the third day. On the first day he asked the attendants: 'Why does not the King desire to have me with him?' They answered: 'He is overcome by drink'. He took a brick and placed it upon a second brick. They went and told it to Solomon, who explained its meaning to be, 'Go and give him more drink'.[136] Next day he asked again, 'Why does not the King desire to have me with him?' They answered, 'His food presses him (he has eaten more than was good, suffers from indigestion)'. Thereupon Ashmedai took the one brick from the other and laid it upon the ground. They went to tell Solomon of it. He interpreted it to indicate: 'Take off from his food (give him less to eat).' At the end of three days he entered Solomon's presence. Ashmedai took a reed, measured up four cubits, threw it before the King and said: 'When this man (Solomon) will be dead, he will command in this world no more than four cubits, now thou hast subjected the whole world and yet thou wert not satisfied until thou hast subjected me too'. He answered: 'I require from thee nought but the stone Shamir which I need for the building of the Sanctuary'. Ashmedai: 'That stone was not given to me; it was given over to the Prince of the Sea; and the latter has surrendered it (given it in charge) to the woodcock to whose oath he trusts'.[137] Solomon: 'What is he doing with it?' Ashmedai: 'He

---

[135] Therein again no one who was unprejudiced could find a "devilish laughter"; as Grünbaum rightly says, anyone would have laughed at the sorcerer working miracles while unconscious of the treasure beneath his feet.

[136] There is nothing but kind solicitude in this action. He is concerned about Solomon and offers his medical advice.

[137] "Who is trustworthy to him" (the cock to the prince of the sea)—(1) who trusts in the cock not to violate the oath he has made to keep it well, or: (2) who is faithful to the Prince as to the oath.

takes it to the mountain which knows no habitation, puts it on the peak of the mountain, etc. etc.'

Benaiah asked Ashmedai: 'Why didst thou bring the blind man back to his way on seeing that he strayed from it?' Ashmedai replied: "In heaven it was proclaimed concerning him that he was a perfectly righteous man, and whosoever did him a kindness would partake of eternal salvation (lit.: would have a merit in or for the world to come).' Benaiah: 'And why didst thou restore the drunkard to the right way on seeing that he strayed from it?' Ashmedai: 'It was proclaimed concerning him in heaven that he was a perfect villain, and I did him a kindness[138] in order that he might eat his deserved punishment in the world to come[139].' 'Why didst thou weep on seeing the merry wedding?' 'The husband was (is) to die in three days and the wife will have to wait thirteen years for the levirate of his young brother".

Benaiah: 'Why didst thou laugh on hearing a man ordering from his boot-maker shoes for seven years?'

Ashmedai: 'This man had not seven days to live, and he ordered shoes for seven years'.

Benaiah: 'Why didst thou laugh on seeing the sorcerer perform witchcraft?'

Ashmedai: 'The sorcerer was sitting upon a royal

---

[138] Did something to calm, benefit him.

[139] Grünbaum translates: "damit er noch länger auf der Welt bleibe", taking it in the sense of "finishing his world", "his course of life". See infra. The expression is somewhat ambiguous and to understand it fully we must refer to the theory according to which the perfectly wicked man, who has some small merit, is allowed to reap the benefit of this merit here, so that all his punishment is reserved for the world to come. Literally: "that he should eat this world". It seems to mean, "This man is really a wicked man and this kindness was shown to him in order that he should eat his deserved punishment fully in the next world," as R. Solomon Edels has it; or that he should enjoy the reward for his good deeds in this world ("eat, enjoy the world"); his life is saved in order that the full punishment of his wickedness, unmitigated by the good deeds already rewarded maybe meted out to him in the world to come. In favor of Grünbaum's explanation speaks only the fact that it does not say, as in the preceding answer: "And whosoever did him a kindness would partake of eternal salvation", i. e. the drunkard was to receive his reward in future life.

treasure. Let him show (he ought to have shown) witchcraft (to discover) what is beneath him'.

Solomon kept Ashmedai with him until the sanctuary was built...

One day he stood with him alone and he said: 'He is to him as the strength (or horns) of a wild ox' (Numbers 24.8). תועפות are the ministering angels and ראם are the demons. 'What is your advantage over us?' asked Solomon. Ashmedai: 'Take off the chain from me and give me the ring and I shall show you what it is'. When Solomon did so, Ashmedai swallowed the ring and extended one of his wings to the heavens and the other to the earth and hurled Solomon a distance of 400 parasangs.

Solomon went continually about begging and claiming to be the rightful King of Israel. None believed his story, until the Sanhedrin made inquiries and heard that Benaiah was never called to the King and that the King in his sexual pleasures transgressed all the laws, asking the women of the harem to come to him during the period of menstruation and lying with his mother. Also that he never uncovered his feet (Ashmedai had the feet of a goat).

Thereupon they began to believe Solomon's story and gave him a ring and a chain with the name of God inscribed upon it. Therewith he entered the room in which Ashmedai sat on the throne and the latter flew away.

The fear of him, however, remained in Solomon's heart and hence 'Lo, the bed of Solomon, sixty heroes surround it, of the mighty ones of Israel; all are girt with swords, trained in war, each has the sword on his thigh, because of the fear in the nights' (Cant. 3.7-8)."

Ashmedai's evil nature harbors no fundamental or consistent animosity against man, he is a mere scoundrel, making full use of his opportunities. There is not one act related of evil for the sake of harming man.

(C) PUNISHMENT OF SOLOMON

Jerus. Abodah Zarah 39: "On the day when Solomon took the daughter of Pharaoh, the angel Gabriel descended, thrust a reed into the sea, mire came up, a big forest grew up, and there, later on, Rome was built."[140]

Jerus. Sanhedrin 20: "When Solomon had transgressed the laws concerning the duties of a King, (Deut. 17.16, 17) an angel descended, assumed his form, deposed him and sat on his throne. Solomon was reduced to frequenting synagogues and houses of learning, where he kept saying, 'I Koheleth *was* king over Israel in Jerusalem.' Thereupon people told him: 'The King is sitting in his palace'. They beat him (for his "lie") and gave him lentils. To this refers his complaint: 'This was my portion from all my labours'".[141]

(D) ASHMEDAI IN "TOBIT"

Here Ashmedai is a sensual demon who, in love with the bride, kills off all her husbands as they approach her and is punished by Raphael, after having been driven out and fled into Egypt. Raphael, the Archangel, binds him. (Tobit, ch. 8.)

Of importance point with regard to Ashmedai is (1) the fact that he is sent by God to punish Solomon's pride. See Grünbaum *Ges. Auf.*, p. 59ff. That Ashmedai is las-

---

[140] It is difficult to imagine anything that would be more catastrophic in the history of the Jews before and after 70 C. E. than this creation of Rome, the most terrible, most relentless enemy. The Roman tax collectors, with legions to support them, committed all possible atrocities and immoralities besides bleeding the country white. Thus the Talmud takes a very decided attitude as to King Solomon's shortcomings.

[141] This version helps to emphasize the contrast between Ashmedai and Aeshma. It is an angel who by God's command came down to chastize Solomon, because he had acted against the Law.

civious is due to the conception that he has שעיר—legs, the שעירים (he-goats) being always connected with immorality, among all nations. (2) He is not a מזיק, but a rascal. (3) For Arab. versions see Grünbaum, also August Wuensche, Der Sagenkreis vom geprellten Teufel.

Chapter 7

(Genesis 6.1–4)

THE FALL OF THE ANGELS

A. Originals of the Story

Vendidad III.24: "O Maker of the Material World, thou Holy One! Which is the first place where the Earth feels sorest grief?"

Ahura Mazda replied: "The seizing[142] of Arezura, O holy Zaratushtra, when upon it the daevas rush, meeting there from the caves."

Yasna 915.46: "And thou didst cause, O Zaratushtra, all the demon-gods to vanish in the ground who aforetime flew about this earth in human shape and power."

30.6: "And they rushed together unto the demons of Fury that they might pollute the lives of mortals."

Haurvatat and Ameratat

Both words are originally abstracts (Fr. Spiegel, *Eran. Altertumskunde*, II, 39.40). *Haurvatat* means 'wholeness'—in one place it is identified with *huyyati*, good life, thus it comes to designate the sum of all pleasures of life; without any spiritual significance modern Parsees see in him the

---

[142] F. Spiegel: Seizings (*grevaya* = akin, *gerew* = foetus) may mean conception. The Huzrarah translation interprets this to refer to the sexual intercourse between Druyas and Daevas. Arezura seems to be a proper name, its root being connected with words meaning envy and jealousy. See his notes pp. 83–84. Darmstetter translates: "It is the neck of Arezura", which is "a mount at the gate of hell whence the demons rush forth."

God of the waters. Ameratat='immortality', then weakened into longevity. Neriosengh identifies him with the Guardian of fodder herbs.

According to Bundehesh, Haurvatat and Ameratat are genii which cause food to be more tasty; they are also charged with providing the souls of the pious with pleasant food as soon as they enter heaven.

In the Vedas 'Sarvatati' means something like 'Freedom from hurt'; Ameratat does not occur in them, but it is probably coeval in development with Haurvatat.

Although, according to the above, these two spirits seem rooted in Indo-European soil, it is remarkable that Harut and Marut appear in the Koran II.96. Iran and Babylon no doubt met frequently, but in the Babylonian myth Haurvatat and Ameratat are too vague for any more definite conclusion to be drawn.

Rivāyet Yasna 915 (46) (Translated from the Persian text in Spiegel, *Comm.*, II, 96). "After 3000 years Zaratushtra the Esfanteman[143] was sent and he spread the Religion. Before his coming the Daevas had gone into the world in human shape (in the form of man and woman fairies). And the Daevas took the women from their husbands and they met in sexual intercourse. When Zaratushtra the Esfanteman brought his religion into the world and made it evident, this band (form) of Daevas were broken up and disappeared.

"Henceforth, if they want to commit a sin on earth they can no more appear in the shape of man, but (they do so) in the form of donkeys, cows and the like (beasts)."

All these stories were in the air. From Egypt, from Babylon they reached popular fancy and it is not unnatural that the vagueness in the terms of Gen. 6.1–4 caused these legends to be connected with the text and almost to

---

[143] = The man who speaks in riddles or parables.

make people forget its proper meaning. The insistence of the Rabbis has saved it from becoming modernized by foreign lore.

Probable Origin

1. That divine beings, even gods, have sexual intercourse with women, was a well-known view, nay, a creed of Hellenistic religion. συνουσία in this sense is mentioned in Josephus, *Antiquitates*, XVIII, ed. Niese, 65ff. See Reitzenstein, *Poimandres*, 228 ff., also 308 ff.

"Amon" sleeps with the queen and foretells greatness to her son just conceived. That "Amon" was not a god does not matter. The existence of the view is proved. Wiedemann, *Herodot*, II, 268 mentions that the emperors of a new dynasty were believed to have been produced by the intercourse of their mother with a god.

Yet the god only creates ἀρχὰς τῆς γενέσεως. Similarly Samael did not quite create Cain, he contributed only the divine part in him.

2. *Ibidem*, 141: "Isis to obtain secret wisdom has gone εἰς Ὁρμανουθὶ ὅπου ἡ ἱερὰ τέχνη τῆς Αἰγύπτου μυστικῶς κατασκευάζεται."

It is obvious that this refers to ἱερὰ τέχνη τῆς χημίας, as Plutarch would say, and that εἰ Ὁρμανουθὶ stands for 'a sanctuary'.

There, first a low god, then the angel Anmael, desired to unite with her, but she demands as price of her love τὴν τῶν ζητουμένων μυστηρίων παράδοσιν. Anmael—who is Chnum—agrees to do so, but causes her to swear that she will betray this secret to none but her son."

As Reitzenstein remarks in his note, the late Jewish imitation has preserved the following characteristics: *Two* angels, who had been sent to the earth, seek the love of a virgin; she promises herself to *one* on condition that he betray to her the secret name of God. For the story see Shemhazai and Azael. Anmael is of course a late addition (with Reitzenstein). For the genius of Jewish folklore it is characteristic to observe the way in which this heathen theory is transformed and purified. Though by no means in harmony with Jewish conceptions, this story is divested of the features most revolting to the mind of the Jew.

In Egyptian lore there is the notion of sexual intercourse between god and man (god and woman or goddess and man). In this 'ecstasy' man receives the highest sanctity, the divine $\delta\acute{v}\nu\alpha\mu\iota\varsigma$; his soul receives the $\sigma\pi\acute{\epsilon}\rho\mu\alpha\ \theta\epsilon o\widehat{v}$. In its Jewish form this intercourse is clearly labelled a sin; the angels who attempted it are punished, the woman who resisted it is rewarded.

The Slavonian Enoch ignores the Jewish Calendar, while it regards as of divine origin the Julian Calendar and the Christian Easter Calendar, including lunar epacts, which we first meet in the 3rd century C. E., and the 532 years cycle, which is not found elsewhere till the 5th century.[144]

Enoch 6.1 ff. "And it came to pass when the children of men had multiplied that in those days were born unto them beautiful and comely daughters. And the angels, the children of heaven, saw and lusted after them and said to one another: 'Come let us choose wives from among the children of men and beget us children.' And Semyaza[145]

---

[144] Dr. Charles had supposed that the reference to the 532 years cycle was one of a number of late interpolations. Mrs. Maunder holds that it is easier to believe in a late author. She calls attention to the Historiated Bibles which characterized the Bogomils. That the present work is Bogomilian is, she maintains, proved by the presence of the legend of Satanail. Her final conclusion is therefore that the book is a Bogomil work written in Bulgaria between the 12th and 15th centuries.

[145] Bousset and Charles speak of confusion, because Semyaza is leader in 6.1 while Azael is chief in other places. That is due not so much to a confusion as to the fact that there must have been a story of two angels, the number of which was increased in later lore. Of the two, one had the same right to leadership as the other. Schwab, *Dictionnaire d' Angélologie, s. v.*, identifies Aza with Semyaza or Shemhazai of the later accounts (Abkir).

who was their leader said unto them: 'I fear ye will not indeed agree to do this deed and I alone shall have to pay the penalty of a great sin.' And they all answered him and said: 'Let us all swear an oath and all bind ourselves by mutual imprecations not to abandon this plan but to do this thing.' Then sware they altogether and bound themselves by mutual imprecations upon it. And they were in all two hundred who descended in the days of Jared on the summit of Mount Hermon[146] and they call it Mount Hermon because they had sworn and bound themselves by mutual imprecations upon it."

Enoch 7: "And all the others together with them took unto themselves wives and each chose for himself[147] one and they began to go in unto them and to defile themselves with them and they taught them charms and enchantments[148] and the cutting of roots and made them acquainted with plants. And they became pregnant and they bare great giants whose height was 3,000 ells, who consumed all the acquisitions of men."

8.3: "Semyaza taught enchantments and root-cuttings,[148] Baraḳiyal astrology.[148]"

Enoch 10: "And the Lord again said to Raphael: 'Bind Azazel hand and foot and cast him unto the darkness and make an opening in the desert which is in Dudael and cast him therein. And place upon him rough and jagged rocks and cover him with darkness and let him abide there for ever and cover his face that he may not see light. And on the day of the great judgment he shall be cast into the fire. And heal the earth which the angels have corrupted.... that all the children of men may not perish through all the secret things that the Watchers have dis-

---

[146] With Hermon חרם and Jared ירד cp. מחלון וכליון in Ruth and also Amos 4.3 ההרמונה which, as the commentaries show, was very variously interpreted. Hermon may thus have suggested itself as the place where sin would be committed, an evil place.

[147] But see the Jewish sources, according to which they chose more than one.

[148] The 'secrets' of the Egyptian and Persian original.

closed and have taught their sons.[149] And the whole earth has been corrupted by the works that were taught Azazel: to him ascribe all sin.'

And to Gabriel said the Lord: 'Proceed against the bastards[150] and reprobates and against the children of fornication and destroy (the children of fornication and) the children of the Watchers from amongst men... Go, bind Semyaza[151] and his associates who have united themselves with women so as to have defiled themselves with them in all their uncleanness[152]... Bind them fast for 70 generations in the valleys of the earth, till the day of their judgment and of their consummation... In those days they shall be led off to the abyss of fire to the torment and prison in which they shall be confined for ever."'[153]

Jubil. 5: "And it came to pass when the children of men began to multiply on the face of the earth and daughters were born unto them that the angels of God saw them on a certain year of this jubilee that they were beautiful to look upon; and they took themselves wives of all whom they chose, and they bare unto them sons and they were giants. And lawlessness increased on earth...

And against the angels *whom He had sent upon earth*, He was exceedingly wroth and He gave commandment

[149] There are three distinct sources of these passages: (a) Magic, etc. from the original source, see above. (b) Corruption from Gen. 6, applied to the angels. (c) Combination of Lev. 18 to account for the fact that of all the angels Azazel alone is mentioned.

[150] In 7.1 we are told "Each chose for himself one", hence bastards does not seem to have the usual sense, but the special one in so far as 'marriages' between angels and women are unlawful. Jewish tradition speaks of the immoral excesses of the stronger race with the daughter of the weaker who—as the text has it—"took themselves women of all they chose" and corruption there means sexual crimes. This corruption in Enoch is divided between the intermarriage and the teaching of magic and astrology.

[151] See Jellinek, *Beth Hamidrash*, II, Pseudo-Jon. Gen. 6.4.

[152] This 'uncleanness' may be levitical or relative, women being unclean as compared with angels, or the angels approaching them during the period of their menstruation, when no Jew should come near them.

[153] It is difficult to find the source for this, unless the various passages in the prophets are combined. Imagination no doubt plays a great rôle here. In Mohammedan accounts the angels suffer only up to the time of Resurrection, and there is no statement about the future. With the impunity of the children of the Watchers cp. the impunity of Uzza (Hebrew Enoch in *Beth Hamidrash* 4, Abkir).

to root them out of all their Dominion, and He bade us to bind them in the depths of the earth and behold they are bound in the midst of them and are kept separate. And against their sons went forth a command from before His face that they should be smitten with the sword and be removed from under heaven."

Ib., 4.15: "And his name was called Jared, for in his days the angels of the Lord descended on earth, those who are called the Watchers, that they should instruct the children of men and that they should do judgment and uprightness on the earth."

Ib., 5. 22: "And he testified to the Watchers who had sinned with the daughters of men; for these had begun to unite themselves so as to be defiled with the daughters of men."

It is wrong to speak of Enoch 6 as the source of the passages in Jubilees. For there is a great difference between them which cannot be explained away. Let me just repeat what I have said before that the Jewish conception of angels—as ministering to God in heaven—does not admit of their indulging in gross sins. Hence angels of God in Jewish lore could never have gone to earth *because* they lusted after the daughters of man.

This is what they do according to Enoch 6. But Jubilees tells a different tale. The angels were sent down, as often they were in Bible times, this time with the view of instructing the sons of men. And on earth—delaying their return to heaven—they become subject to earthly temptations and passions and sin. In heaven they could not do so.

We must thus say that either Jubilees used a different source or, if Enoch supplied it, there was a deliberate alteration, of the text to bring it into harmony with Jewish ideas. Since the story of fallen angels reached Jews (see above) indiscriminateiy, I see no reason why just Enoch should have supplied it to the author of Jubilees.

Enoch 64: "I heard the voice of the angel saying: 'These were the angels who descended to the earth and revealed what was hidden[154] to the children of men and seduced the children of men into committing sin'".

B. Possible Interpretations

The following questions present themselves:

(1) Who were the Bene Elohim?

(2) Who were the Benoth Haadam?

(3) Who were the Nephilim?

There are three explanations possible, or four. We shall discuss one after the other. (1) Bene Elohim means "angels". They are so named with reference to their divine nature. The Bene Elohim or Bene Elim sing the praises of God, take part in the court of Heaven, appear to man to deliver him (Ps. 89.7; Job 1.6; Dan. 3.28). It is with special reference to their angelic nature that they are given this name; as messengers of God and as executors of His will they are called 'Mal'akim' (messengers). The introductory chapter on angels has made it clear that in the common consciousness of the Bible as well as of later Judaism they were celestial not only as regards their dwelling-place but also in their nature. In the whole of the Hebrew Bible there is no statement pointing to the moral deficiency of any angel. And in the whole range of not only 'orthodox' literature, but of undiluted Jewish Folklore angels appear as impeccable, divine beings. Not faultless, nor omniscient, but just

---

[154] The communion between man and god (in the Egyptian account generally) had the teaching of magic as a consequence. If not magic then secrets. Since the angels sinned, all their deeds must have been evil, hence magic and astrology "corrupted the earth". For details see Enoch 69.

and good by nature and beyond human passions.[155] Hence it is only in such strata of rabbinic literature as show distinctly foreign influence that this interpretation is to be found, and even there only as a haggadah among many. Hellenistic Judaism knew it (Josephus, *Antiquit.*, I.3; Philo, *De Gigantibus*, ed. Wendland, the Pseudepigrapha: Enoch, Jubilees, XII Patriarchs). From what we said above about the angels in the New Testament it is obvious that this interpretation will have found entrance there (Jude, 6; 2 Peter, 2.4). And the manner in which they are mentioned shows that in the mind of the preacher there was a definite, well-known story, in keeping with the general conception of angelical nature. The Church Fathers based their view necessarily also on the New Testament. (The difficulties which arose owing to the conflict between the former and the description of the Hebrew Bible, also authoritative to the Fathers of the Church, are dealt with in the remarks on Gregory the Great.)

What speaks for the identification of Bene Elohim in this passage with Angels? Apparently the contrasting 'Daughters of men'; though in some sense this begs the question. Further, apparently the fact that the offspring of the connection between Bene Elohim and Benoth Haadam are described as Giants by the almost unanimous opinion of all commentators. On second thought these things fall to the ground. I am not even convinced that the passages of the New Testament referred to above originally meant or indeed even now mean to apply to our passage. The Lucifer problem is much more prevalent in early Christian Literature than the "Angels" of 6.4, and "the angels which kept not their first estate but left their own habitation and whom he hath reserved

---

[155] Codex Gaster, Samaritan Commentary to Genesis. 1184 f; 142b, 143b. הנפלים הענקים והלכו אחריהם בני השלטונים ובאו את בנות האדם. בני אלהים בני השלטונים והם אשר היו בזה הזמן שלטים בין החייבים.

in everlasting chains under darkness unto the judgment of the great day" as well as "the angels that sinned" whom God did not spare, appears to me to refer much rather to the Lucifer story as misinterpreted by the Church, as described frequently in the New Testament ('And the devil who by reason of pride and arrogance fell from heaven, punished by God; himself and his fellow angels who rebelled with him'). That from an early time 'angels' was only one of several interpretations will follow from what I shall have to say under (2).

To examine the reasons:

(a) As has been said before, 'Bene Elohim' refers to angels as ethical superhuman beings; when they are rebuked they are 'mal'akim'.

But Elohim stands also for judges, for rulers of men. Therefore Bene Elohim need not mean angels at all. In Psalm 82 b: "I said, ye are Elohim, and all of you sons of the Most High", the term distinctly refers to human beings. In 73.15: "If I had said, I will speak thus; behold I had dealt treacherously with the generation of thy children," the pious ones are called "the sons of God," not to mention Deut. 14.1; Exodus 4.22.

(b) As to the apparent contrast, it is not convincing either. 'Adam' as opposed to a better class of man, or simply meaning 'other men', 'remainder of men', occurs in Isa. 43.4 ('I shall give Adam (men) for thee') and in Jeremiah 32.20 ('which didst set signs and wonders in the land of Egypt, even unto this day; both in Israel and among other men, ['Adam]'). Comp. also Ps. 73.5: "Neither are they (the wicked) plagued like Adam=other men". Thus the contrast does not prove anything as to the nature of Bene Elohim.[156] We find Adam *opposed* to other beings, human as Adam himself.

[156] The daughters of man were 'tobot'. With Ehrlich *Randglossen* I, p. 28 we may take it to mean "of large stature". Hence the giants. For 'tob' in this sense cp. I Sam. 9.2; 10.23.

What proof remains for Bene Elohim as angels? The fact that pseudepigraphic literature and to some small extent rabbinic lore have accounts of fallen angels (or descending angels) who lust after, and sin with, the daughters of men. Now again there are two possibilities. Either that the text as we have it before us originally meant to convey the idea, or that the ambiguity of the term served as a peg to hang on it the foreign lore for which it seemed suited. If we succeed in proving the existence of an early non-Jewish extra-biblical legend of that fact, we shall have made way for the plausibility of this theory.

Strange to say that parallel with this interpretation another one is to be found. It becomes quite clear that if we assume that Gen 6.1 speaks of angels, all the theories of fallen angels as part of biblical lore must be based on this passage, and therefore any translation of Bene Elohim other than 'angels' cuts away the ground beneath these legends. And yet we find that the text is taken to speak of anything but fallen angels, while the existence of such beings is at the same time upheld. This may be due either to the fact that the Lucifer story was somehow or other connected with it, that the fallen angel of the Devil would commit all sorts of excesses, or that a foreign tale, more or less fitting into the text, was at an early time introduced into the consciousness of the writers of stories of fallen angels.

Bene Elohim may also mean the Spiritual Children of God, as the examples above show. Our text then would indicate that these pious and exalted sons (or children) of God, through some cause or other, left their previous estate—and did what? mixed with the daughters of men, to whom giant children were born.

Of any crime to provoke God's punishment there is little trace in the text. Unless we suppose that there was some law forbidding intercourse between the children of God and "men", of which there is no evidence. The theory invented to make both ends meet does not prove of any avail. Till now, it is said, the respective families of Seth and Cain had developed without mixing. Now they did intermarry, consequently the purity of the Sethites became influenced, to its disadvantage, by the wicked Cainites, and this was the wickedness of it. The pure and innocent Sethites bequeathed to their offspring their unspent virility (hence 'giants'), the Cainites supplied technical knowledge, arts of armoury, etc., hence the men of renown, who were the heroes of old, reaped the benefit from the accomplishments of their respective families. Hence their arrogance, hence the punishment (of verse 3), and the warning, and the deluge. This view is just as untenable as the first one. It does not account for the punishment by any textual evidence. It does so by supplying a background for the working theory. It is not said or even alluded to in Genesis 4 or 5 that the Sethites were any better than the Cainites or that the Cainites were any worse than the Sethites, or that they were forbidden to intermarry, while the text renders it pretty clear that God must have considered the mixture of Bene Elohim with Benoth Haadam an offence to be severely punished. There remains accordingly but one interpretation. It would have to account for God's anger, it would have to be seen clearly in the text that the taking of wives must be a crime, in short it must be both reasonably in harmony with the general conception of angels in the Hebrew Bible, and clear in itself. This interpretation is given in Onkelos and goes all through rabbinic literature. Onkelos reads: "The sons of the princes (Mighty Ones)[157] saw the daughters

[157] רברביא gives a general sense rather than a definite etymology. This term in Aramaic denotes equally 'big' (Gen. 12.17), 'older' (*ibid.* 25.23), 'Prefect' (Exodus 18.1), and may here mean people bodily strong (Giants), or 'politically' strong

of men that they were beautiful and they took themselves women of all in whom they found pleasure."

This is philologically defensible. The sin lies not in the marriage, but in the fact that "they took unto themselves as women in whomsoever they found pleasure". This appendix is eloquent enough. They took the women of all classes, grades, states, single or married, in whom they found pleasure, who just aroused sensual passions in them. We know that these men (sons of God) were mighty heroes, they would have giant sons. The sons of the mighty, at whose mercy the poor are, would naturally be stronger in body and health, in the animal part of man. These sons of the mighty, by transgressing all laws of nature and God, by sheer sexual savagery, corrupted the whole race of man, shortened their years and brought about their downfall—the deluge. There is thus supplied the *motif* for God's anger and punishment.

Very interesting and plausible is the explanation of Nahmanides:[158] "Adam and Eve are the children of God, since they were created by Him, not born of a woman. Their children retain this name. The later races are no longer so strong. Since they lived long, they might have chosen from the tenth generation, they, the giants, from the children of woman-born weaker ones."

The most remarkable thing about these various versions is that they appear parallel. This seems to indicate that there were originally two independent stories, somewhat akin, which were brought near each other by the features common to them. We have spoken already of the fact

---

(tyrants). Targum Pseudo-Jon., a veritable storehouse of all sorts of legends, has רברביא too, and this fact strengthens the view that the Jews at any rate interpreted Bene Elohim as 'earthly tyrants'. When Pseudo-Jon. introduces Shemhazai and Azael into verse 4, he apparently does so because of the word נפילים, which, combined with the Persian saga, then rather common, seemed to give sense.

[158] Moses ben Naḥman (1195–c.1270), talmudical and biblical scholar, mystic, hilosopher.

that the whole story of fallen angels depends—for the exegete at any rate—on the translation of 'Bene Elohim'. This fact throws an interesting side-light on the theory of Rabbi Simeon bar Yohai's authorship of the Zohar. In Genesis Rabba he is very severe on those who translate the passage as referring to angels; it must be taken, he maintains, to refer to sons of the mighty. In the Zohar the story of fallen angels—based on Gen. 6.1–4—occurs some twenty times, and even in those portions which scholars are inclined to consider basic and ancient. Now the fact must not be denied that a difference is possible between פשט, the exact translation, and דרש, the homiletical exegesis, which—haggadistically—lays more stress on the idea than on the text, which now and then suffers violence from the ingenuity of the preacher. But it never goes so far, unless for a definite reason, that what one rejected and denounced as פשט he should himself handle, accept, develop in דרש. Nor can we assume that the disciples of Rabbi Simeon bar Yohai would have taught that to which their master so severely objected. It must then be a very late hand that inserted it. And since it occurs too often to be explained away as *an* (one) interpolation, it shows that a great part of the Zohar is very much younger than Rabbi Simeon bar Yohai—comp. what is said about the similar difficulty by Augustine. And see also sub Gregory's Haggadah.

Who are the Benoth Haadam?

According to the first interpretation they are all the daughters of men who sinned with the angels. According to the view that Bene Elohim are the Sethites they are the shameless daughters of Cain about whom scandalous stories are told. See texts. According to the third interpretation they are the helpless women, both married and unmarried, of the weaker caste, whom the strong and savage men took "according as they were pleased with them."

Shemhazai and Azael according to Midrash Abkir[159] (full text)[160]

Rabbi Joseph was asked by his pupils, "What is 'Azazel'?" He said: "When the generation of the deluge arose and served idols, the Holy One blessed be He, was grieved. Immediately two angels arose, Shemhazai and Azael, and said before Him, 'Lord of the Universe, have we said before Thee before Thou didst create the world, 'What is mortal man that Thou art mindful of him?' He said: 'And what shall be with the world?' They replied: 'Lord of the Universe, we would have been satisfied with it.' He said: 'It is evident and clear before Me that if ye dwelt on earth the evil inclination would rule you, and ye would be (harder) worse than the sons of man.' They said: 'Give us leave, let us dwell with the creatures and Thou wilt see how we shall sanctify Thy name.' He said: 'Descend and dwell with them'. At once they corrupted themselves (did corruptly) with the daughters of man who were beautiful, and were unable to subdue their desire (passion).

Immediately Shemhazai saw one girl,[161] whose name was Istahar. He set his eyes on her and said, 'Grant my desire!' She replied: 'I will not grant it until thou teach me the Shem Hammeforash, by means of which thou ascendest to heaven, at the moment (hour) thou pronouncest (rememberest) it.' He taught her that Name, she pronounced it, ascended to heaven, without having sinned (dealt

---

[159] A Midrash extant in excerpts on Genesis, and Exodus, in pure Hebrew. All the homilies end with אמן בימינו כן יהי רצון hence the name. Older than Rabba Rabbeti, cited already in the 11th cent. See Strack, *Einleitung*, p. 209.

[160] See Gen. Rabba 8.5. This identification of Shemhazai and Azael with Truth and Justice is rather arbitrary. We must assume that it is due to a sort of reconstruction of history to suit a definite theory.

[161] *Only* Sh. lusts after her. Cp. Judges-version.

corruptly). The Holy One blessed be He, said: 'Because she has kept herself far from sin, go ye and fix her among the seven stars in order that she may be mentioned among them for ever. And she was fixed in the Pleiades.[162]

When Shemhazai and Azael saw that, they arose and took women[163] and begat (as) sons Heeva and Hiyya.[164] And Azael was (set) over the kinds of cosmetics (colors) and over the kinds of ornaments of (appertaining to) women, which (the ornaments, מִפְתִּים) persuade the sons of man to think of (committing) sin.

Immediately Metatron[165] sent a messenger to Shemhazai[166] and said to him: 'The Holy One blessed be He is about to destroy His world and to bring a deluge (over) the world.' He began at once, weeping continually and grieved, because of the world and of his sons.

Then follows a description of their voracity and dream. When he told them that the Holy One blessed be He, was about to bring the deluge and that only Noah and his sons would be saved, they cried and wept. He said: 'Grieve not, your names shall not cease from this world. For whenever (He) shall decree evil, or people shall lift up stones or ships, they shall mention your names "Heevah! Hiyya!" They acquiesced.'

Shemhazai repented and hanged himself between[167]

---

[162] But see the Venus episode. (Cp. Yalḳuṭ 132, 273: Azael still walks about, pursuing women.)

[163] Though נשא אשה is (in the Mishnah and Gemara) the technical term for 'marrying', a glance at Gen. 6.4 will make it obvious that 'marry' is not intended here.

[164] Heevah and Hiyya as interjections—"Woe! Ah!", the issue of the wicked will cause many a sigh. Nay, in every groan and sigh they will be 'represented' and 'expressed'.

[165] It is interesting to note that in the Midrash on the Death of Moses, Metatron is a partisan of Samael; an interesting explanation of his name may be found in Ziuni 39a: M. = guide of the way.

[166] Note that Sh. plays the chief role: Sh. sees the girl, teaches her, receives the messenger, etc.; cp. with Enoch.

[167] See Deut. Rabba (near the end) for a reference to *Uza and Azael*, two angels of whom it is told that they went down from the Divine Presence on high and lusted after the daughters of the lands and corrupted their way on earth until God suspended them between earth and firmament.

heaven (and earth), head downwards and feet upwards, and he is still suspended, in repentance, between earth and heaven.

Azael[168] did not repent, and he still abides in his corruption to lead astray (persuade) the sons of man by means of women's cosmetics. Therefore did Israel offer up offerings on the Day of Atonement, one ram unto the Lord to atone for the children of Israel, and one ram to Azazel that he carry (away, sustain) the iniquities of Israel,' And this is 'Azazel' of the Law."

Nephilim

Franz Delitzsch, in his New Commentary on Genesis (I, 232 f), gives to נפל the meaning "bastard", adducing the German "Fallkind" as an analogous expression; in German, too, this word means "Bastard". There is little to be said against this, because ἅπαξ λεγόμενα must be allowed any meaning which fits the passage in question, unless evidence to the contrary is brought forward. Gesenius (before him Luther) would have it that Nephilim means 'degenerate giant races'; Numbers 13.33 may lend itself to this view, but our verse does not. It has also been connected with פלא to account for the wondrous size, but that is unlikely. It is better to indulge in no theories and to say that 'giants' is likely to be the meaning, though the etymological history of the word is obscure.

AUGUSTINE ON GENESIS 6.1–4

De Civitate Dei XV, 22 end. 23: ..."This charity or attachment the sons of God disturbed when they forsook God and were enamoured of the daughters of men. And

---

[168] Origen's famous 'heresy' that even Satan will be finally redeemed, may not be uninfluenced by the final peace between Man and Serpent (Targ. Jon. Gen. 3.14) as well as by the version of our story, according to which the two angels, or one of them, will be suspended between heaven and earth only until the Day of Judgment.

by these two names (sons of God and daughters of men) the two cities[169] are sufficiently distinguished. For though the former were by nature children of men, they had come into possession of another name by grace. For in the same Scripture in which the sons of God are said to have loved the daughters of men, they are also called angels of God; whence many suppose that they were not men but angels...

"There is a very general rumor that sylvans and fauns had often made wicked assaults upon women... And that certain devils, called Duses by the Gauls, are constantly attempting and effecting this impurity is so generally affirmed... that I dare not determine whether there be some spirits embodied in an aerial substance, who are capable of lust... But certainly *I could by no means believe* that God's holy angels could at that time have so fallen nor can I think that it is of them the Apostle Peter said, 'For if God spared not the angels that sinned, but cast them down to hell'... I think he rather speaks of those who first apostatized from God, along with their chief, the devil, who enviously deceived the first man under the form of a serpent... But the same Holy Scripture affords the most ample testimony that even godly men have been called angels (Mark 1.2 and Mal. 2.7).

"But some are moved by the fact that we have read that the fruit of the connection between those who are called angels of God and the women they loved were not men like our own breed, but giants; just as if there were not born even in our own time men of much greater size than the ordinary stature. (As an instance he cites the gigantic women of Rome, at whom crowds came to marvel.)

"Giants therefore might well be born, even before the sons of God, who are also called angels of God, formed a

---

[169] The earthly and the heavenly, "formed by two loves, the earthly by the love of self, even to the contempt of God, and the heavenly by the love of God even to the contempt of self". Book XIV.28.

connection with the daughters of men, or of those living according to men, that is to say: before the sons of Seth formed a connection with the daughters of Cain.

The words 'There were giants in the earth in those days *and also after that* when the sons of God came in unto the daughters of men' prove that there were giants both before 'in those days' and 'also after that'.[170]

"But that those angels were not angels in the sense of not being men, as some suppose, Scripture itself decides. For when it had first been stated that the angels of God saw the daughters of men that they were fair and they took them wives of all which they chose, it was immediately added, 'And the Lord God said: My spirit shall not always strive with these men for that they are also flesh.'[171] For by the spirit of God they had been made angels of God and sons of God; but declining towards lower things, they are called *men*, a name of nature not of grace; and they are called flesh, as deserters of the Spirit.

"The Septuagint[172] indeed calls them both angels of God and sons of God, and Aquila 'sons of God'. But both are correct. For they are both sons of God, and thus brothers of their own fathers, who were children of the same God; and they were sons of Gods, because begotten by gods, together with whom they themselves also were gods, according to that expression of the Psalm, 'I have said, Ye are gods and all of you are children of the Most High.'

"Let us omit, then, the fables of those scriptures which are called apocryphal...For though there is some truth in these apocryphal writings, yet they contain so many false statements that they have no canonical authority.

---

[170] This depends on the translation of אֲשֶׁר; 'because' seems to give best sense, as it would account for the birth of giants, but not "before."

[171] One cannot but admire the ingenuity of Augustine, for the next sentence allows the above interpretation according to any view of the definition of Bene Elohim.

[172] See Frankel, *Vorstudien*, p. 67.

The writings produced under the name of Enoch are not genuine... just as many writings are produced by heretics under the names both of other prophets and under the name of apostles. There is therefore no doubt that there were many giants before the deluge and that these were citizens of the earthly society of men, and that the sons of God who were according to the flesh the sons of Seth, sunk into this community when they forsook righteousness."

Who Are the Nephilim?

It seems they are the product of the 'marriage' between Bene Elohim and Benoth Haadam. It seems, we say, because, though we have translated אֲשֶׁר = 'because', it must be admitted that another interpretation does not appear quite wrong. "The Nephilim were in the earth in those days and also afterwards". That may mean in those days before the mixing of the Bene Elohim with the Benoth Haadam and also afterwards when the children of this connection also were giants. But, (translating it 'for' or 'because') the Nephilim are the product, and since the Bene Elohim and Benoth Haadam continued being together, they produced generations of Nephilim.

The ancient versions (LXX, Samaritan, Onkelos, Peshitta) took it to mean "giants". It appears to be a very old word with a definite meaning attached to it. Grammatically it could be the plural of נָפֵל (cp. פְּסִילִים), though this נפל has a different meaning. That נפל suggested a great many things is perfectly clear in itself, and the passage by the ambiguity of some of its terms and names seemed to invite the imagination of scribes and minstrels to regale itself by finding all possible stories in it. It has become the source of many stories, some read into the text.

"Legt ihr's nicht aus
"So legt ihr's unter.

And some, originating elsewhere, were based upon with this text as their raison de'être.—

Onkelos: גִּבָּרַיָּא is ambiguous, it may mean hero as well as giant. He translates the Hebrew נברים by the same word.

Midrash Genesis Rabba, 26, 4.: "Seven Names were they called: 'Nephilim' (here), 'Emim' (Gen. 14.8; Deut. 2.10), 'Refaim' (Gen. 14.5; Deut. 2.11; 3.11; Joshua 17.15.), 'Gibborim' (6.4), 'Zamzummim' (Deut. 2.20), 'Anakim' (Deut. 1.28; Joshua 14.12, 15;) 'Avim' (Deut. 2.23; Jos. 13.3)

All these names except Nephilim in Genesis (Nephilim of Numbers 13.33 is no exception) refer to ancient races, living in the mind of the Jew as giant savage men. There is no connection with deities in any passage, save in the above, if misintepreted. This alone shows clearly that to compare the Nephilim with Greek legends of Titans is to forget this essential difference. But, to come back to the Midrash: "They are called '*Emim*' (Fear-inspirers) because their fear—אימה—falls upon all; '*Refaim*' (Courage-melters) because whosoever sees them becomes weak like wax; '*Gibborim*': R. Abba in the name of R. Johanan said, "The brain in the head of one of them was 19 cubits (long)"; *Zamzummim*—R. Jose son of Hanina of Naditmon said: They were excellent[173] in battle. '*Anakim*'. "The Rabbis said they were so called because they wore many ornaments (or because they were of tremendous height reaching the course of the sun with their neck: ענק=عنق, whence העניק to put something on one's neck). In this sense, which seems the right one, and in harmony with the interpretations of the other names, it is taken by M. Tanḥuma, Genesis 42, and in other Midrashim, as well as in the Babylonian Talmud, Sotah 18b.: "R.

---

[173] μέγιστοι, orig. מגיסטי.

Aḥa said: they are so called because they surrounded the course of the sun, saying: 'Bring down rain.' 'Avim'—they caused the world to be desolated and they too were banished...as it is said[174]: 'An overthrow, overthrow, overthrow shall I make it.' (Ezek. 21.32). R. Eleazar b. R. Simon said: They were called 'Avim' because they knew the (dust) soil like a serpent, and in Galilee a serpent חויא—is called עויא.[175] 'Nephilim'—because they caused the world to fall and they fell from the[176] world and because they filled the world with[177] untimely births by reason of their immorality.'

Pesikta Rabbeti 34: "If Uza and Azael, whose body was fire, sinned, when they had descended to earth, how much more (shall) we?"

'Sihon and Og are descendants of the fallen angels.' This statement is derived from Nu. 16.33: 'There we saw the Nephilim the sons of Anak.' Tradition knew that Sihon and Og were giants.

Pugio Fidei 728. Quoting Midrash Rabba Rabbeti; see Epstein, *Magazin*, 1887: "And the Bene Elohim saw the daughters of man that they were fair." With

---

[174] עוה in Aramaic = to be desolate, Pael or Aphel: to make desolate; Syr. צדי, Pael and Aphel: to lay waste. עוה in O. T. Hebrew means to sin, to act perversely, but also to destroy, overturn (Isa. 24.1).

[175] For the various readings עוי, ואן see the Dictionaries; also for the meaning of 'knowing the soil', being able by tasting it to determine its quality—like the serpent, who will be the expert in dust.

[176] The Hebrew is not unambiguous. For 'being banished from the world, perishing', the technical term is אבד מן העולם or active הוציא מן. As it stands, it may well refer to human beings who destroy the world by immorality and, drowned in the deluge, fall themselves from the world. On the other hand the similarity of expression in Jud. 6f. 'which kept not their first estate', or in Fathers of the Church, 'fell from their first estate', is too striking to be neglected.

[177] Popular eymology has been at work here. The נפל untimely birth, the plural of which would be נפלים has suggested it; immorality would be punished by "untimely births". Nephilim develops in two directions; it becomes the name of a mighty man, a virtuous hero; in Ruth Rabba 39c, where Boaz is one of the Nephilim, it degenerates into demonology. רוח בן הנ' 'the spirit of the demon B. H.' In Babli Bekor. 44b, Sifra Lev. 10.5, it means 'nervous breakdown' or 'stupidity'; it is also the name of a species of Lizard, born 'from the eggs of a tremendous crocodile'. The name of the Messiah בר נפלי has no connection with it. It means 'son of the cloud'; cp. νεφέλη. We thus have three interpretations of 'Bene Elohim': (1) Angels; (2) Sethites; (3) Sons of Aristocracy.

regard to all sins is the Holy One blessed be He patient, except in matters of immorality.[178] Whence is this maxim derived? From the fact that 'And the Bene Elohim saw, etc.' is immediately followed by 'I shall wipe off man.'

R. Joseph said "The angels saw that the Holy One blessed be He was grieved that He had created man. Immediately on seeing that, two angels, whose names were Shemhazai and Azael, stood up before Him and said to Him: 'Lord of the Universe, did we not say unto Thee at the time when Thou didst create Thy world, 'Do not create Man; as it is said, What is mortal that Thou shouldst be mindful of him, and the son of man that Thou shouldst visit him?' God replied to them: 'But what shall become of the world?'[179] They replied: 'We shall work in it.' He replied: 'It is revealed and known before me that if you were in their World with the Evil Inclination having rule over you as it has over man, you would be worse (lit. harder) than they.' They said: 'Give us permission to dwell with the creatures and Thou shalt see how we shall be sanctifying Thy name.[180] The Holy One blessed be He replied: 'Herewith I have given you permission to do so!' They went down immediately and the Evil Inclination prevailed over them. When they saw the daughters of man that they were beautiful, they went astray after them, unable to quench their lust.

To this refers, 'And the Bene Elohim saw', etc. Shemhazai saw a virgin[181] whose name was Esthera, he put his desire on her (lit: gave his eyes on her) and said to her:

[178] Martini has זוֹלַת which is a mistake, זְנוּת being the proper reading, or better זְנוּת like גַּלוּת. There are several mistakes in our passage, due to negligence, ד' instead of ר' etc.

[179] i. e. the world was a fait accompli before man; created for man (see Rashi Gen. 1.1). Or: If I now destroy man, what shall become, etc.?

[180] The sanctification of God's name is a law and duty peculiar to Judaism. Deeper than anything else it has influenced Jewish life, both public and private. A wicked, dishonest deed is not only abominable for its wickedness but especially because it is a desecration of the divine name. This conception is associated with all laws of Israel.

[181] רביתא not רבה as the text has it; 'maid'.

'Do what I want from you ('Hearken unto me'). She replied, 'I will not do so until thou teach me the Shem Hammephorash'[182] whereby thou ascendest to heaven when thou pronouncest it.[183] Immediately[184] he taught her the name, she pronounced it and thereby ascended to heaven. The Holy One blessed be He said: 'Because she had kept herself apart from transgression, I shall make her an example[185] to be remembered for ever. 'And God placed her immediately among the seven stars of the Pleiades. When Shemhazai and Azael saw this they began[186] to marry (take) women who bore children unto them."—Rabbi said: "Could it occur to you that flesh and blood could come near the angels? Is it not written: His servants are a flaming fire? (Ps. 104). Our story, however, teaches us that when the angels had fallen[187] from the place of their holiness in heaven, the Evil Inclination gained sway over them as over the sons of men, and their forces and their strength were reduced to (the level of) man, and they became clothed with the clod of the earth, as it is said, 'My flesh is clothed in worms and in the clay of the earth (Job 7.6).'"

R. Zadok said, "From them were begotten the Anakim who walk about[188] in the arrogance of their heart and in their pride putting forth their hands to all manner of robbery, violence and shedding of blood:[189] as it is said, 'And

[182] The secret name, 'set apart', not the 'ausdrückliche Name'. In the Egyptian prototype, too, it is a secret thing.

[183] זכר to pronounce, in Hebrew הזכיר; cp. מאן דכר שמיה 'who mentioned his name?'

[184] מיד is idiomatic in Midrashic tales.

[185] דוגמא = δεῖγμα, 'example', 'parable'.

[186] Lit: 'they arose and'.

[187] They had not 'fallen', but had come down by God's special permission; unless we take מקום קדושתן spiritually, 'from the degree (rank) of their heavenly saintliness. In this form it would account for the two different phrases in other versions.

[188] מלכין misprint for מהלכין.

[189] The shedding of blood is not referred to in Midrash Abkir. Moral corruption is what they are usually charged with. Only in Mohammedan accounts (the Zohar episode) do they shed blood; indeed, there they commit the three cardinal sins of Islam: Immorality, Drinking of Wine, Shedding of Blood. The parallel is interesting and may justify important inferences as to the date of this version.

there we saw the Nephilim,[190] the sons of Anak, who come of the Nephilim; and we were in our own sight and so were we in their sight as grasshoppers'" (Num. 13.32.).

The Nephilim were in the earth...

They (the Sages) have taught: "Shemhazai[191] begat two sons, Ḥivvah and Ḥiyyah, they married women and begat as their sons Sihon and Og. It was told about Shemhazai that he repented and suspended himself head downwards between heaven and earth because he had no means of defending himself[192] before the Holy One blessed be He, and until this day he is suspended in penitence between heaven and earth.

But Azael did not repent and he[193] was appointed over all sorts of cosmetics and all sorts of ornaments of the women which captivate (mislead) men into transgression, and he still remains in his corruption, and for this reason Israel bring sacrifices and give one lot for God that He may wipe away the sins of the children of Israel and one lot to Azazel[194] that he may carry[195] the sins of Israel, hence it reads (Lev. 16): 'And Aaron put lots on the two he-goats..

[190] Printed three times נפלאים; the printer or scribe had perhaps פלא in his mind. This etymology has not been wanting either. See on Nephilim, Philological Note.

[191] It is Shemhazai who begot these sighing monsters, it is Shemhazai who repents. Azael was prevented from doing so because folklore had begun to connect him with Azazel.

[192] "Because he had no opening of the mouth before the Holy One, blessed be He." In the Hebrew Bible this expression occurs only in Ezekiel 16.23; 39.21, but it is common in later Hebrew. In the liturgy (Prayer for the New Year) we ask for "freedom of speech for those who wait for Thee."

[193] Who appointed him? "The angels taught magic and the arts of adorning" both in Islamic and in early Persian lore. This is derived from there. Egyptian stories have 'Chemistry'.

[194] The argument is vicious. What is the meaning of this story? Azazel sins and therefore he gets an offering? He is to carry the sins of Israel? How? The School of Rabbi Ishmael connected the Azazel with the laws against immorality read in the afternoon service of the Day of Atonement. That appears much more sensible but it does not cover the whole ground. That on the Day of Atonement the most common sin should be especially mentioned, is not at all unintelligible, even if we disregard the Azazel interlude. That Azazel is not Azael is clear. But just as in the case of Nephilim, the similarity of the names had suggested a connection between the two.

[195] לסבול 'carry,' not 'carry away', rather—take them upon himself. But what should a lascivious fallen angel do with these sins? And why should he of all beings in the world be entrusted with them? After all ἀποπομπαῖος is simpler, clearer and therefore truer. Ḳimḥi's עז אל 'the goat went hither' is ingenious enough.

one he-goat for the Lord....and the other one stood alive before the Lord to be sent to Azazel, into the wilderness' ".

Yalḳuṭ 44: 'Aza and Azael'. "Shemhazai is mocked by Ishtar but he seduced the daughters of man. As a punishment he is suspended head downwards between heaven and earth. Azael still walks about on earth seducing women by ornaments and in disguise.

Azael is Azazel to whom the children of Israel offer a he-goat on the Day of Atonement that he may carry away their sins.[196]

Zohar *ad locum*: 'The Bene Elohim, etc. (Gen. 6.1–4). Rabbi Jose said: "They are Uza and Azael......And these rebelled above[197] and God cast them down and they became substantial on earth and remained there and could no more depart from there. Afterwards they[198] went astray after the women of the earth...And until this day are they alive, teaching man magic. They begat sons called Anakim, Gibborim. And these Nephilim[199] were called 'Bene Elohim.'"

Jastrow 923b: (1) '*Giants*', Gen. R.26. (2) בן נ׳ *demon;* רוח בן נ׳ *nervous prostration.*; (3) *Species of lizards.* (4) *Untimely birth* (no plural); (5) נפילה *falling.*

---

[196] This corresponds to the statement in Yoma 67b: Azazel—'he is so called because he atones for the sins of Uza and Azael.' The passage from the Pentateuch read in the afternoon of the Day of Atonement was chosen because it contains injunctions against incest, reminiscent of Uza and Azael.

[197] This is a combination of various sources. They rebelled—either by objecting to the creation of man, or by accusing Adam wrongly—or 'they rebelled' is to account for their descent.

[198] Not one alone.

[199] It is not clear who 'they' are. Are the Nephilim their children, thus 'Sons of Divine Beings' or are the fallen angels Nephilim? Should perhaps the fact that the Nephilim still are called 'Sons of God' account for a somewhat similar theory in Gregory respecting the inalienable divine nature of even the fallen Satan? The Zohar has such a mass of ancient thought in it that an inference such as suggested above, may not appear quite unjustified.

C. History of Interpretation

(A) Jewish

Rabbi Simeon b. Yohai. (Second Cent. c. e.)

Gen. Rabba 26.2: "And the Bene Elohim saw, etc." Rabbi Simeon b. Yohai called them 'The sons of the Judges.'[200] Rabbi Simeon ben Yohai cursed all who say that Bene Elohim means 'Angels.'[201] In explaining this passage as referring to the immorality of the sons of the mighty judges he said: "A breach that does not come from the upper classes is not a real breach......Why then were they called Bene Elohim? Because they lived long (had a long life), free from trouble and chastisement."[202]

"That they were fair." Rabbi Judah (fourth century) said: The Hebrew reads טבת which may be the singular (טבח), to indicate that when the maid was being adorned[203] to meet her husband, a Big One[204] would come in and lie with her first. "That they were fair" refers to the maidens (as above). "And they took themselves wives"—this

---

[200] Judges are called 'Elohim' Exod. 21.8; cp. also the passage mentioned in the preface.

[201] This sage consistently explains Exod. 14.19 in the Mechilta *ad loc.*

[202] This interpretation, as Theodor remarks, is independent of Rabbi Simeon ben Yohai, but I believe it shows at any rate that in the opinion of Rabbi Hanina and Resh Lakish they were "happy, strong men."

[203] כי טבת that she was being adorned. Syr. טיב.

[204] A Big One, one of the sons of the Judges, of the רברביא.

means women married already to someone else... See *ibid.* for the bestiality of the Big Ones.

Nahmanides *ad locum*: "Rashi and Midrash refer it to the sons of the Judges. Thus Scripture tells us that the Judges whose business it was to judge among them, were themselves committing violence with none to prevent them[205]." As Gen. R. puts it: "Whenever you see immorality spreading, the doom of mankind (in form of pestilence, etc.) is fast approaching."

Genesis Rabba 26.4: "And also afterwards when the Bene Elohim went in unto the daughters of man." R. Berachiah said: "A woman going abroad would see a youth, lust after him, would go to lie with him and bring forth a youth as (great, strong, lusty) as he."

This too helps to show that the interpretation of the passage by the Rabbis had nothing to do with angels. Bene Elohim suggested 'angels', and that angels occasionaly were treading earthly soil is abundantly told in the Bible. Considering especially the antiquity of Genesis Rabba, its failure to mention anything about fallen angels who lusted after and begat children with, the daughters of man, seems eloquent enough.

Before R. Simeon b. Yohai, Tryphon objected to this interpretation. But it is evident that Christian scholars did uphold that view and were eager to find it established in the text, hence our Rabbi's sharp rebuke addressed to all who would introduce foreign lore into the Torah (Cp. Justin *Dial.* 79).

Josephus (*Antiquitates* I, 13) too heard of the angels' story and his mind apparently did not find anything wrong in this interpretation.

---

[205] Somewhat similar are the stories according to which the Angels' plea: 'What is man, etc.' caused God to show them that they too would sin if they were flesh and blood. They were then ordained judges and they did misuse their power. This was taken over by Mohammedan tradition, see *ibid.*

Pseudo-Jonathan[206] has both the Jewish and the non-Jewish interpretation. Bene Elohim are[207] the sons of the Mighty Ones, and the daughters of man are adorned and shamelessly provoke immorality; but this interpretation is forsaken in verse 4. "Shamhazai and Uziah (In Ginsburger, Azael)[208]—they are fallen ones from heaven, and they were on the earth in those days and also afterwards when the sons of the mighty came in unto the daughters of men and bare children unto them, and these were called heroes of old, the famous men."

Midrash Hane'elam Gen.6.—"Nephilim".—"The Nephilim were in the earth in those days."[209] "They are Adam and Eve who 'fell to the earth' without either father or mother."

Midrash Ruth. "Uzah and Azael were on earth, the Bene Elohim were not on earth. R. Judah said: 'The Bene Elohim were also called "Nephilim." 'Bene Elohim.' R. Hiyya said: 'The Bene Elohim are simply the sons of Cain.[210] Cain was the product of the serpent[211] unlike a human being....thus also his sons. And for this reason

---

[206] See Ch. Heller, Jerus. Targum, New York, 1921.

[207] There is something wrong with this text. For Shamhazai and Azael are out of place; those who cohabit with the daughters of men, both verse 1 and verse 4, were mighty men. Where do the two angels come in? There is no indication in the text of Pseudo-Jon. of their having had anything to do with the women. I believe it ('Sh. and Azael...they are the fallen ones') is a late gloss of some one who had heard this unorthodox story and was desirous of recording it here.

[208] See Schwab's Vocabulaire d'Angélologie who identifies Shamhazai with Azael. That the story of fallen angels does not originate from Gen. 4.6, but goes back to Babylonian Mythology, Schrader has demonstrated in Die Keilinschriften und das alte Testament, 3te Aufl. sub Weltschoepfung.

[209] This view is important for its tendency. Bene Elohim were not on earth. This does not amount to a denial of events to that effect elsewhere in the Hebrew Bible, but to the idea that angels could not have been on earth in the capacity and fleshliness ascribed to the Bene Elohim of our passage. This Rabbi represents the Jewish conception of this affair, forming a link between Rabbi Simeon ben Yohai and the opponents, both Jewish and Christian, to this invasion of foreign lore.

[210] As a rule the 'daughters' are the wicked ones; here the order is reversed, because Eve's first born, 'gotten with a divine being', was a son, Cain.

[211] The functions of Samael and the Serpent here appear rather confused. It is Samael who was with Eve, though the Serpent too is mentioned in this connection. But it is necessary to remember that wherever the Serpent is described as lusting after or sinning with Eve, he appears to act spontaneously. In allowing Samael to speak through his mouth he acts as his servant, but in all other matters this co-operation is not mentioned.

they were called Bene Elohim.—And they were also called Nephilim, because the serpent was Samael's messenger and the taints of lasciviousness originating in Eve's posterity from Samael...caused them to degenerate...Because they fell (lit.: 'came down') they are called Nephilim."

Another version (late) Zohar I, 184. 'And the Bene Elohim saw.'[212] "This refers to Uza and Azael who rebelled against (accused) their lord[213] and the Holy One, blessed be He, caused them to fall from the holy place above...and on coming down they became solid[214] bodies from the air (atmosphere) of the world...they clothed themselves in the air of the earth...and behaved like human beings... thus they were called 'Men'[215]...having been cast down, they assumed a human constitution, became unable to fly and having remained seven days on earth could no more return to their original abode."

A different stratum, Zohar I, 183: 'And the Bene Elohim saw the daughters of man'. "They (the Bene Elohim) are the Nephilim, for those angels, mixing with outside forces which were not holy, fell from their holiness[216] and below, on earth, they mixed with the forces of the nation; as it is said, 'And they took to themselves women.'"

Pirke de R. Eliezer, ch. 22: Rabbi said: "The angels who fell[217] from their holy place in heaven saw the daughters of

[212] Cp. 'Shamhazai and Azael' and 'Objection to Creation'; these two motifs are concocted here.

[213] מריה referring to Adam is puzzling. But see sub Schatzhoehle. That the Zohar does take it so is clearly stated on the following page, see col. 2.

[214] גלם to mantle, cover; גולמא shapeless matter; thus substance, and here: assume substance.

[215] This seems to me to account for the next verse, where God's punishment refers to man only. According to the present interpretation it extended to the angel who had become man.

[216] From this text a different narrative—or a varying source—might be obtained. In another version we find God sending angels to prove to them their weakness once in flesh and blood. The angels, thus descended, would not have fallen from heaven, but—as our text has it—from their holiness. When speaking of fallen angels, this difference ought not to be overlooked, though in effect the two versions may mean the same.

[217] Goes back to Enoch, yet they fall first and then only see and lust after the daughters of men.

the generations of Cain[218] walking about naked, with their eyes painted like harlots, and they went astray after them and took wives from among them, as it is said, 'And the sons of Elohim saw the daughters of men that they were fair; and they took them wives of all that they chose.'"

Rabbi Joshua said: "The angels are a flaming fire, as it is said (Ps. 104.4): 'His servants are a flaming fire,' and fire came with the coition of flesh and blood, but did not burn the body; but when they fell from heaven, from their holy place, their strength and stature became like that of the sons of man, and their frame was made of clods of dust, as it is said (Job 7.5): 'My flesh is clothed with worms and clods of dust.'"

Rabbi Zadok said: "From them were born the Giants, who walked with pride in their hearts and who stretched forth their hands to all kind of robbery and violence and shedding of blood, as it is said (Num. 13.33), 'And there we saw the Nephilim, the sons of Anak,' and it says (Gen. 6.4): 'The Nephilim were on the earth in those days.'"

Rabbi Joshua said: "The Israelites are called sons of God, as it is said, 'Ye are the sons of the Lord your God' (Deut. 14.1). The angels are called sons of God, as it is said: 'When the morning stars[219] sang together and all the sons of God shouted for joy' (Job 38.7).

And while they were still in their holy place in heaven, these were called 'Sons of God', as it is said, 'And also after that when the sons of God came unto the daughters of man and they bare children to them, etc.'"

Rabbi Levi said: "They bare their sons and increased and multiplied like a great reptile, six children at each birth."

---

[218] These Cainites are esp. valuable to the Sethites v. Cainites interpretation. Cain's birth (as due to Samael) may have caused this story.

[219] The LXX paraphrases 'My angels'.

(B) *Christian*

Justin Martyr, *Apol.* II, 6: "God delivered the care of man to the Angels whom He appointed over man. But the angels transgressed His order and fell into intercourse with women and begat sons, who are those that are called demons; and moreover they henceforth subjected the human race to themselves; in part by magic writings... and they sowed among men murders[220], wars, adulteries and intemperance and all kinds of vice."

Ephraem 46.4. "The angels were not called at any time sons of God that they might not confuse their name by reason of their natures."

Sons of Seth

Ephraem supports his interpretation by arguing: (a) If the production of giants requires the intervention of angels, then the production of dwarfs must be supernatural. (b) If angels could make women mothers, then devils could also and so would have imitated the birth of a virgin. (c) If God had intended the race of angels to be propagated He would have made them female and male. (d) The sons of Seth are called "sons of God" because they dwelt apart on Mount Hermon and devoted themselves to a life of angelical devotion and contemplation.

Why Did the Angels Fall?

Irenaeus I.2: "And the angels who had transgressed and become apostates and impious and unjust and iniquitous men God sends into eternal fire."[221] See *ibid* 12f.

Lactantius *De origine erroris*, II, 15. "God sent angels

---

[220] Whence has Justin Martyr derived the angels' committing of murder? Perhaps from "All flesh had corrupted its way." This expression, according to Jewish tradition, refers to moral looseness. Justin "proves" his haggadah by reference to Isaiah 30.1–5; Zech 3.1, Ps. 96.5, Job. 1.6, etc.

[221] Lucifer and his host. 'Ignis' here for the bottomless pit.

to guard and serve the human race.[222] As these lived with men, the most false lord[223] of the earth beguiled them by sheer intercourse to sins and polluted them through copulations. Then they fell down to earth, having been refused admission to heaven because of their gross sins. Thus did the Devil[224] make out of God's angels his own satellites and ministers. They, however, that were begotten by these, were neither angels nor men,[225] but had some intermediate nature. They, however, were not received by the lower creatures, just as their parents had been refused admission into heaven.[226] Thus two kinds of demons[227] were created, one heavenly, the other terrestrial."

Athenagoras XXIV, *Defence of the Christian.* "One group rebelled and was cast[228] down to earth through the air. Some of these fell in love with women and begat the giants with them. Henceforth the souls of the giants

---

[222] This is a feature unknown to the Haggadah. It occurs in the Mohammedan traditions. Midr. Abkir tells us of God's testing two angels on their own request by sending them to earth to withstand there all attempts of the Yezer Hara'. The angels which protect man, as a rule (in the Haggadah) do so from heaven, coming down only occasionally. Cp. Gen. Rabba on 32.25, Talm. Babli Ḥulin 91.2. Their descent (see sub Athenagoras) accounts for the fall of impeccable beings.

[223] This also is new, though by no means surprising. The sum and source of all temptations is "dominator ille terrae fallacissimus" and by sinning they would naturally come into his power. As to their incapacity for re-entering heaven, see sub Athenagoras. How could they fall "tum," when their sins must have been committed on earth. Or in mid-air?

[224] There is undoubtedly a Lucifer motif. It is he who makes his whole order fall with him, 'making them his satellites'. The mere fact of their sinning would not make them 'his ministers' though it would subject them to him.

[225] Cp. the Samael-Cain legend. Cain was born of Samael by Eve, hence combined in him the natures of man and angel. Hence he is called by some "Ben Elohim" and the Bene Elohim are his sons; as against the usual interpretation.

[226] That again is a new development, akin to Shedim theories. But it seems a piece of Lactantian Haggadah.

[227] This may be due to the non-identification of Nephilim with Bene Elohim, 'Nephilim' suggests 'genus terrenum'.

[228] That appears to be another account, or a new combination of the Lucifer and Nephilim legend. It is noteworthy that the angels pass some time in the air, beyond heaven's influence, before they are capti amore mulierum. Here again the right conception of angels has effected this argument: "Angels cannot sin."—"Admitted, but that is only in heaven; the atmosphere outside the blessed region is infected with all sorts of sins and temptations and our angels who were captivated by illicit love for the daughters of man, spent some time outside heaven."—The same feeling may have produced the saying (Jewish Haggadah) that angels who spent more than 7 days (or a month) outside their celestial abode, were unable to return to it. It occurs in Zohar, a. l.

are the demons which stray about the world and entice men to errors and into the greatest sins of idolatry and lust.

Why did the angels fall?—Some of the angels were faithless. Their leader[229] with many others was driven from his estate because of negligence and improbity. Some of them were captured by an illicit love for women and with them begat giants. The souls of the giants are the demons which entice men into lust. God created angelic virtues (and offices). Some of the angels fulfilled their parts duly and received their meet reward (probably the tutelage of the human race). Others were degraded because they had neglected and abused their office."

Justin Martyr, *Pro Christ. ad Senat. Roman.*: "Why did the angels fall?—The guardianship over man was from the very beginning of the world entrusted to the angels. But they were conquered by their love for women, fell into many other errors,[230] and after they had with these women begotten giants, they reduced the human race to servitude. After their immoral conduct with the women the demons inspired men with so much terror that they called upon them[231] as if they were gods, and ultimately came to believing them divine beings."

Clemens Alex.: "Why did the angels fall? Because of negligence.[232] Some angels having been incontinent were overcome by lust and therefore came down from heaven.—

[229] Here we have a combination of the two principal accounts of the Fall of the Angels. What is most interesting is the fact that according to the Fathers of the Church the first fall happened before the creation of man, when Lucifer fell and man was created to replace him and his legion, while the second fall took place before the deluge, leading up to it. Here they are combined.

[230] See *Apologia*, II, 6. The crimes were committed after the descent.

[231] This is a curious interpretation of Gen. 6.1–4. The 'Nephilim' were on earth before the angels had come down, they were the product of the angels and committed immoral deeds. The Nephilim (the product of the Bene Elohim and Bene Ha-adam) were 'once upon a time' called 'Dei', then believed to be such. Now the Bene Elohim were angels, according to the present interpreter. Their children were sons of human mothers. Yet they were such terrible demons that they were believed to be gods.

[232] This is too vague to enable us to infer whether the Lucifer or the Bene Elohim episode is referred to. The former occurs more commonly.

These angels, stooping to passion, betrayed secrets to women."[233]

Athenagoras, *Plea for the Christians*. "Those angels who have fallen from heaven and the giants which are the demons who wander about the world, perform actions similar; the demons to the nature they have received,[234] the angels to the appetites they have indulged."[235]

Recognitions of Clement A. III 297.—Further developments—. "Lustful angels teach man that demons, by certain magical invocations could be made to obey men." This is prominent in Moslem literature.

(C) Mohammedan

Harut and Marut

Tabari, *History*, I, 169. On the authority of Ibn Abbas. "Between Noah and Idris there was a period of a thousand years. There were two divisions among the sons of Adam, such as dwelt in the mountains and such as dwelt in the plains. The mountaineers had beautiful men, but their women were ugly, while the reverse was the case with the people living in the plain. Iblis came to one of the 'plain dwellers' in the form of a young man and accepted employment with him. He took a shepherd's pipe and played on it. People had never heard anything like it before then. The news (of his music) went round and people came in turns to listen to him. They appointed an annual festival for the purpose of gathering round him. And the women would decorate themselves for the men and people would come down to them. One of the mountaineers happened

---

[233] A combination of the last two extracts gives the main features of the story as it appears in pre-Jewish sources. These main features (women-lust-secret) are characteristic. It is the Bene Elohim account.

[234] Human and divine, being the offspring of angels and mortals.

[235] The angels have freedom of will, just like man, hence their sin, the result of which is the giants.

to be present at the annual festival and saw the beauty of the women. He returned to his people and informed them of it. They came down to the women, stayed with them and adultery became common among them. To this refers Ḳuran 33.33:

'And abide still in your houses and go not in public decked as in the days of your former ignorance but observe prayer and give alms and obey God and His apostles. God only desires to put away filthiness from you as his household, and with cleansing to cleanse you.'"

Another version on the authority of Al-Hakimi: "Between Adam and Noah were 800 years. The women of that period were very ugly and their men very handsome. The women would thus have lustful designs on men, wishing each of them a man for herself for intercourse. To this refers the above verse."

Ibn Abbas: "Within the lifetime of Adam the number of his sons and grandsons reached 40,000 and Adam saw among them adultery and drinking of wine and wrong-doing. So he admonished them that the children of Seth and the children of Kabil (Cain) should not intermarry. The sons of Seth imprisoned Adam in a cave and set a watch over him so that none of the sons of Adam could reach him.

"Those who would come and for whom he asked pardon were the sons of Seth. A hundred of these handsome Sethites said, 'Let us go and see how the children of Cain have fared.' So a hundred of them came down to the pretty women of the sons of Cain, the women kept the men and they stayed with them for a long time. After some time another group of a hundred Sethites said, 'Let us go down and see how our brethren have fared,' so they came down from the mountains to them and they too were kept by the women. Then all the sons of Seth came down and the sin became common. And they intermarried and they mingled with each other and the children of Cain multiplied until they became Kings[236] in the earth and it is they who were drowned in the great flood of Noah."

The Magic of Harut and Marut

Ibn Abbas, Tabari, I, 3, 40: "*Ma* here means 'not.' God says 'Magic was *not* sent down to Harut and Marut,' i. e. The sense of the verse is: 'The devils believed not, they taught men sorcery and not what was sent down to the two angels at Babel, Harut and Marut.'"

The next passage shows that Ibn Abbas' reading, or rather translation, is untenable, for "Those two taught no one until they had said, 'Verily we are a temptation'" implies that they taught something forbidden, while Ibn Abbas would cause us to infer that the devils committed wrong in teaching men sorcery *instead* of teaching them a lawful thing, viz: what was sent down to Harut and Marut. The tendency of taking '*ma*' in the sense of 'no' is clear enough, the angels as angels could not teach anything forbidden. *Vide* Hassan's reading الملكين 'Kings'. Ibn Abbas has both, the story of fallen angels and the attempt to explain away a passage clearly at variance with the conception in Islam of their impeccability. The same holds good with regard to Augustine and perhaps also with R. Simeon b. Yohai. They would not give up the story, though denying its being derived from the Holy Book.

Tabari *Comment* I, 341, 10. "The devilish art of magic was taught by two *men*, Harut and Marut. The two angels of this verse are Gabriel and Michael and the passage is

---

[236] This is the second interpretation of Genesis 6.1-4. We found it developed in Augustine's *De civitate*, in Isaac of Antioch. The present is a rather embellished form of the story and it is idle to endeavor to find sources for the individual developments. The essentials are taken over from Christian lore. Two parties, one good, one evil. Mixture forbidden, yet effected. Product: Giants, which, like the Kings here, correspond to the 'men of renown, the mighty men of old.'

said to mean that not (*Ma*) Gabriel and Michael had taught the people magic, but it is a devilish art taught by two men. The Devils teach magic to Harut and Marut (acc.) who in their turn teach men."

Ibid.6. "Magic is an art of the Devil and they teach it to people in Babel and those who teach it are two men, one of them is called Harut and the other Marut." This explanation equally does violence to the text and its tendency is the same. Cp. the Cainites vs. Sethites as against the Fallen Angels interpretation.

Tabari I, 340: "There were two kinds of Magic, one taught by the devils, one by the angels sent down."

On the authority of Ibn Wahb., 341–42. Tabari defends the traditional view (as represented by the text of the Koran) that Harut and Marut were two angels, for 'God creates both, good and evil.'

This, however, fails to do justice to the nature of angels as generally conceived.

The Book of the Creation and History. Ed. Cl. Huart, El Balkhi, III, 15 ff.: "The Moslems tell the history of Harut and Marut in diverse versions. Certain legend-tellers relate that when God the most High wished to create Adam He said to the angels, 'I am going to place a substitute on earth.' They replied, 'Wilt Thou place there one who will do evil therein and shed blood, while we celebrate Thy praises and sanctify Thee?'[237]

"When Adam was created and his posterity began to do injury to one another, the angels said, 'Are these those[238]

---

[237] *Sura* II, 28.

[238] Cp. in the Jewish texts: 'Did we not say unto thee, What is mortal man that thou be mindful of him?'—No mistake! Meshnevi (Rosen, 196) speaks of three angels who are sent down to earth, God wishing to show them that in the empire of Satan and carnal lust they would be worse than men, of whom they complain. One of the angels smells danger, retires to heaven and remains a saint. The others commit the sins and are confounded. The woman, as in the other stories, ascends to heaven. Wine, as in the other stories, causes idol-worship and murder, besides betrayal of the magic name.

whom Thou hast chosen as vicars on earth?' God commanded them to take three[239] of the best among them to send them down for the purpose[240] of bringing man to truth. They did so.

"It has been said[241] that a woman came to them and seduced the messengers. They drank wine, killed living beings and worshipped creatures besides God; they taught the woman the Name by means of which they ascended to heaven. She ascended by means of it and was changed into a star, to wit, our Venus.

"It is added[242] that the angels were given the choice between punishment in this and the future world (life). They chose the former, hence they are suspended by the hair in a pit in the land of Babel. The magicians go out to find them and through them inform themselves of the art of magic.

The philosophers give little credit to this legend, especially in what is said of Venus, because she is joined to the party of retrograde stars which God arranged as a pole and support for the universe. Nor do they believe the story about the fornication committed by the angels, to whom God had attributed a long devotion and the ambition of approaching Him. Besides they had not at all a body subjected to carnal passions nor an empty belly for which one should allow such conduct on their part.

"Some persons also say that they were given passions and membra virilia.

"If Harut and Marut were angels as it is alleged, they

---

[239] Perhaps mistake for 'two', as in all other sources. See note 166.

[240] There are two accounts of the purpose in the cycle of these legends. The first, "to justify the ways of God to—angels," justifies His creation by saying angels in human atmosphere would also sin, as they are said to have done eventually. The other, losing sight of this point, remains consistent as to the impossibility of angels committing a sin. Hence they were sent down to correct man. Once on earth, they imbibe human frailties, or become bodily men, etc. etc. El Balkhi speaks out on the second side with no uncertain voice.

[241] Note the sceptical tone, which becomes more pronounced as the chapter goes on.

[242] See Note 241.

should have been sent to show men the different kinds of magic and to put them on guard against them and the painful results of this art, and this to be their only purpose. El Hassan reads "malik" = king, instead of "melak" = angel in the passage Koran 2.96. It is also said that they were two pagans of Babel.

"As for Venus, if she means anything in this story, it is that some men, seduced by her, have worshipped her, just as they suffer themselves to be seduced by Sun, Moon and Sirius (to worship them).

"We are told on the authority of Rabi ibn Anas regarding this legend: 'It was a woman, whose beauty among women was equivalent to the beauty of Venus among the stars. But there is nothing like this in the book of God. It is by such stories that the heretics try to lead astray the hearts. But God is our help.'"

His arguments may thus be summed up: 'The Koran speaks of Harut and Marut, not of Venus. We must either altogether eliminate Venus from traditional stories or we must take her 'seduction of men' to mean that men worship her. The legend is incompatible with the conception of true religion. It is heretical.' El Balkhi is a courageous anti-metaphysician. (It is instructive to compare both Kazwini's definition of angels and the evidence of the Koran itself, which agree with El Balkhi's conception of them as pure ministers of God. This conception is borrowed from Judaic lore. Midrash Rabba Rabbeti, the exception, is influenced by non-Jewish sources. See sub *Pugio Fidei*, note.)

Kazwini, ed. Wuestenfeld, I, 12. "Harut and Marut are the two angels who were punished at Babel." On the authority of Ibn Abbas: "When Adam was cast out of Paradise naked, the angels looked at him and said, 'Oh, our Lord, that is Adam, who had been called into being out of nothing by Thee. Forgive him and do not let him perish.' Then Adam passed by a crowd of angels and they heaped abuse upon him because he had broken the covenant with his God. And among those who reprimanded him were also Harut and Marut. And Adam said, 'O angels of the Lord! Have mercy upon me and do not rebuke me with such bitter rebuke (with menacing words). What has happened to me was decided as a predestined decree of my Lord'. And God tried the two (Harut and Marut), until they rebelled against Him and then they were forbidden to ascend to heaven. When the days of Idris[243] had come, the two angels went to him and told him their story. Then they said: 'Is it possible for you to intercede by prayerful blessings on our behalf so that our Lord may forgive us?' Idris replied: 'How am I to know that God has forgiven you?' They said: 'Just call on God on our behalf. If you see us then, it will mean that your prayer has been accepted; if you do not see us, we are lost.'

"Idris performed the ablutions of the rite and then prayed to God Almighty. Turning after his prayers, he was unable to see the angels and he knew that punishment had been decreed for them. They were transported to the country of Babel and then the choice was given them between temporal and eternal punishment. They preferred the punishment of this world and now they are kept chained and tortured in a pit in the land of Babel, head downwards until the day of Resurrection."

The two outstanding features of Kazwini's form of the narrative are the connection of Harut and Marut with other angels and the absence of any details as to their sins.

---

[243] Idris = Enoch, in another version simply 'a pious man'. The story there is somewhat fragmentary. 'They were forbidden to ascend', when they descended is not said.—The sign of the acceptance of the prayer is new.—Nothing is said about their magic.

These features may be connected so that the one would account for the other. The dramatic motif may be found in the fact of their malicious attitude towards poor Adam; their punishment consisted in God's trying them until they rebelled. (In this we may have a faint reminiscence of the Abkir motif, where the angels fall as a direct consequence of their severe judgment against Adam; or of their arrogant rebuke.)

Mr. Huart has this interesting note: "M. J. Halevy a fait justice, dans le *Journal Asiatique*, IXe ser., t.XIX 1902 p. 146 et suivantes, de l'étymologie proposée jadis par P. de Lagarde et qui rattachait Hâroût et Mâroût a Haurvatât et Ameratât; celle qu'il propose avec reticence et prudence et qui est peu satisfaisante, a l'avantage de ne pas quitter le terrain sémitique seul solide en ce qui concerne Babylon et les legendes qui s'y rattachent. Il faut peut-être voir dans Marsut une survivance du dieu Merodach[244] Mardouk, car c'est dans son temple (tombeau de Bélus, Babil) que se trouvait une 'cellule des oracles' comme à Borsippa et où se rendaient les oracles des Chaldéens, le soin de les prononcer etait specialement confié à deux divinités, Merodach 'Le dieu des horoscopes' et Ao." See also Oppert, *Exped. de Mesopotamie*, I, 178, II, 27: f.

With de Lagarde agree Rückert, Lobeck, Burnouf, see *ibidem*.

Halevy's objections do not seem to be valid. His own explanation is unsatisfactory. The difficulty namely that Harut and Marut are wicked angels, whilst Haurvatati and Ameratati are the opposite, is not as grave as might appear. Harut and Marut, according to Sura 2, 96, are ministers of God. "They hurt none thereby, but by God's permission." Although it must be admitted that in common Moslem consciousness they are evil spirits, even that is

---

[244] I am afraid this is 'peu satisfaisante', Harut and Marut were angels sent down from heaven. But Magic was a later trait in this connection; "arcana" they taught according to almost all accounts.

no real stumbling block. If Moses' sister could become Jesus' mother in the course of her being transplanted from the Jewish to the Arabic Bible, Harut and Marut may well have suffered similar changes. I thus can see no solid objection to de Lagarde's theory, which has the added advantage of being borne out by the names themselves. Or else I should have proposed another solution of the problem, which struck me as I was comparing the various sources. *Yarad* means to descend. The angels came down in the time of *Yared*. *Marad* means to rebel. The angels did rebel. In Arabic *marada* has a similar meaning. Both 'coming down' and 'rebelling' are essential to this story, the descending and the rebelling. *Warada*, it is true, means only coming, but there *yared* may have come in. Haurvatati and Ameratati may have been the originals of Harut and Marut. 'Coming down' and 'rebelling' surely describe them well.

P. de Largarde, *Ges. Abhandlungen*, 15: 'In Harut and Marut I have found the amshaspands Haurvatāti and Ameratāti who are now called Chordād and Mordād. This legend—as may be seen from Gen. 6.1; I Corinth. 1.10, 11—is a very ancient one and preserved only in fragments.'

Allusions to them are very frequent with Moslem poets, the dimples in the cheeks and chin of the beloved ones being compared with the well of Babel wherein Harut and Marut sit captive, teaching Babylonian Magic.

Anahid to mean: 'the sweet one' *ibid*. 9.

Esteira = ast = ἀστῆs, Venus is "starin" with the Syrians. *Analecta* 137, 22; 152, 28.

Zuhrat = 'Αφροδίτη = בלתי = כתי = אנהיד = עסתרות = כוכב נוגהא.

Lagarde 15 ff. בידוכת = Bedukht, either dulhiter-Kosrovidukt or باداختی, having caused misfortune.

עץי bei den טייא.

Ἄζιζος name of Mars in Edessa. Whether any connection with עזא?

Sura 2.96. ".....And Solomon was not an unbeliever; but the devils believed not, they taught men sorcery and that which was sent down to the two angels at Babel, Harut and Marut. Yet those two taught no man until they had said, 'Verily we are a temptation, therefore be not an unbeliever.' So men learned from those two a charm[245] by which they might cause division between a man and his wife. But they hurt none thereby except by God's permission."[246]

Tabari I.341, 10.: "They were two of the angels, and they were sent down (from heaven) in order that they might arbitrate between men; and this was due to the fact that the angels derided the judicial sentences pronounced by human beings. So a woman appealed to them[247] (i. e. to Harut and Marut) for a judicial sentence and they gave an unjust sentence in her favor."

Tabari I, 341, 11ff.: "Then they departed ascending (to heaven), but they were prevented from doing so (i. e. they were not admitted into heaven) and they were told that they must choose[248] between being punished in this world and being punished in the next. So they chose to be punished in this world...So they used to teach men

---

[245] A charm—not in the text. I follow Sale's translation which I found quite faithful to the original.

[246] Note that within this paragraph there are two statements with a tendency. "Yet those who taught no man until they had said, 'Verily we are a temptation, therefore be not an unbeliever.'" They go further than even Satan of the Hebrew Bible. They warn men off. And the second sentence, "But they hurt none thereby except by God's permission." What made these two things necessary? Only the fact that Mohammed had taken over the Jewish conception of impeccable angels. They are sent down from Heaven by God as His messengers, therefore they warn men against the perils of their teachings. They are His angels though on earth, therefore they cannot hurt without His permission. All through the Koran and its commentaries goes this notion, and consequently whenever the story of Eblis' sin is related, it is insisted upon that he was a 'genius', not an angel.

[247] I am under obligation to Professor A. A. Bevan for his help in translating this difficult passage. He says: "We should probably read فحاكيت اليهما امراة. The verb حاف imperfect يحيف is used in the Koran 24.49.

[248] وخير (passive).

sorcery and the condition was imposed upon them[249] that they should not teach any one without previously saying: 'We are a temptation, therefore be not an unbeliever.'"[250]

Various Versions of the Harut and Marut Story

On the authority of Ibn Abbas: *ibid*. 343, 27ff. "God opened the heaven for the angels to watch the deeds of the sons of Adam: when they saw them doing evil, they said, 'O Lord, these are sons of Adam, whom Thou createdst with Thine own hands[251] and Thou madest Thy angels to prostrate[252] themselves before him and Thou taughtest him the name of everything—and behold they are sinning.' God said, 'But if you were in their place you would do what they are doing.' They said, 'Thou art far from imperfections. It would not become us to do so.' Thus they were commanded to elect from among them those who would go down to the earth. They elected Harut and Marut who descended to the earth. God made lawful to them everything that was there except that they were not to acknowledge anybody besides God, not to steal, not to fornicate or drink wine and not to take a life that God has forbidden to take except lawfully. It was not long before there appeared before them a woman to whom half the beauty (of mankind) had been given, her name was Bedukhut. When they saw her they desired to commit adultery with her. She said, 'Not until you join other gods with God and drink wine and take a life and prostrate yourselves before this idol.' They said, 'We are not going to join any god with God.' Then the other one asked to go again to her. She said: 'Not until you drink wine,' which they did, until they became intoxicated and a beggar

---

[249] Read فَاخِذ impersonal passive (Prof. Bevan.)
[250] The tendency sustained, see s. Koran.
[251] See under 'Adam'. That is Jewish.
[252] See sub Eblis. This is Christian doctrine.

came to them and they killed him. When they did this evil that they did, God opened the heavens to the angels. They said, 'Thou art above imperfection. Thou knowest better.' Then God inspired Solomon son of David to give them a choice between the punishment of this world and the next. They chose the punishment of this world and were put in chains from their ankles to their necks, as is the case with the neck of Bactrian camels and they were put in Babel."

Tabari 346, 24: Some read المـلكيـن—this is contrary to the tradition and otherwise wrong.

Ibid. 26: "The prophet had been affected by the sorcery of a Jew. The author thinks that sorcery 'is to make one imagine a thing as different from what it essentially and really is.'"

347, 23: The story of a woman who came to Medina soon after the death of the Prophet and said that she had been to Babel and seen Harut and Marut.

348, 17: 'How Harut and Marut teach men the black art.'

Ibid. 344,8: (a) "When Harut and Marut, the chosen representatives of the angels, descended to the earth, Venus too descended, in the shape of a Persian woman. And the Persians called her Bedukhut (Ibn Abbas)."

"(b) Venus was a pretty Persian who brought a case before Harut and Marut. They tempted her (to commit adultery). She made the fulfilment of their desire conditional on their teaching her the repetition of the formula,[253] which when pronounced, would cause one to ascend to the heavens. They taught it to her. She pronounced it and consequently

---

[253] We have these two versions, the Zohra and the woman version. The former ends with the transformation of the woman into a star, the latter is not concerned with the future of the woman and proceeds to tell of the punishment which befell the sinful angels. Compare with the punishment the accounts in *Pugio* and *Pirke d. R. E.* That Azael is still at large is due to the theory which brings him into connection with Azazel. Where this tendency is absent, both angels suffer equal punishment.

ascended to the heavens and was metamorphosed into a star."

(c) 344, 20. (Kab) "Harut and Marut did all that was forbidden to do before the evening of the day of their descent".[254]

(d) *Ibid.* 26: Kab's fuller version, in essence the same as (a) and (c).

(e) 345,1: On the authority of Al-Suddi. "Man has ten passions which are also given to Harut and Marut. They landed in Babel, used to descend (from heaven) in the morning, ascending (from earth) in the evening. The plaintiff was a woman who had a quarrel with her husband.

Her name was in Arabic: الزهرة
in Aramaic: بيدت
in Persian: اناهيد

To fulfil her condition for allowing them to commit adultery with her they[255] pronounced a judicial sentence against the husband. They went to an old ruin, where she refused to do anything unless they gave her the formula by means of which they ascended to, and descended from, heaven. They told her the formula, she pronounced it and ascended heavenwards. But God made her forget the second one, with the help of which one could descend.[256] She thus remained where she was and God made her a star (changed her into a star)."

Ibid. 345,1: "Abdul ibn Amr used to curse Venus whenever he saw her, saying: 'This is she who tempted

---

[254] The tendency is not clear. It would be clearer, if Moslem tradition taught some time limit for angels to return to heaven, after having descended. But it may perhaps mean that they became evildoers at once so that God's word proved true on the very day they had entered terrestrial spheres, having immediately become subject to human temptation and human frailty.

[255] There is no reason here for singling out one of them, hence both angels lust, sin and suffer equally.

[256] As a rule she asks only for the formula for ascending, her aim evidently being to be transported to celestial regions. But since we are told that she asked for both formulae, it must be explained that God, by making her forget the second, was the cause of her failure to descend.

Harut and Marut.' The angels when trying to ascend in the evening, found they were unable to do so (on account of their sin)."

(f) Al-Rabi, 345, 19: "It was after Adam that men fell into sins. Then angels said to God, Thou createdst man for Thy worship, but, etc...When the two angels descended, it was the time of Idris (Enoch).[257] There was a woman at that time as pretty as Venus among the stars."

(g) Isnad, 346. "On the authority of the Prophet. Harut and Marut were the angels selected by other angels for descending to the earth, as in above version."

(h) Mujahid. The same story as the preceding one, but with more details. The following are the most important modifications:

(1) Venus is the star descended, she appeared to them as a pretty woman, after Harut and Marut had acted as judges between men for some time.

(2) Before the appearance of Venus they used to descend in the morning and to ascend[258] in the evening to the heavens.

(3) The two angels had no desire for women as men have. They showed their naked body (membra) to Zohra and enjoyed it. Then Zohra flew back to her place.

(4) When they found in the evening that they could not fly with their wings, they asked a pious man[259] to pray to God on their behalf, which he did. The prayer being accepted (they ascended to heaven and) were given a choice, etc.

(5) They were sent down to Babel, that is the place of their punishment. It is said that they are hung head downwards in iron chains, flapping their wings.

---

[257] There were yet Enoch traditions. Cp. Jubilees.

[258] Similar things are told in the Haggadah about both Satan and his clownish double, Ashmedai. The latter takes part in the heavenly councils and in terrestrial meetings, the former goes down, observes, tempts, ascends, accuses and as Angel of Death comes down again with the permission to take the life of the guilty man.

[259] This pious man was Enoch and this is taken from the book of Enoch, 72.

Tabari, .p. 341: Tabari thinks that هاروت and الذى—ما وماروت are in apposition to الملكين.

For if otherwise, Harut and Marut would be in apposition with الناس and ما would be negative. If so, Harut and Marut would be either two angels or two men. If they were angels the fact that they deny God and insist on teaching sorcery would be a more serious allegation against them than what is said about their committing the sin and the consequent punishment meted out to them. If they were men, sorcery ought to have disappeared after their death, as they were the only source for knowing it.

Original

Koran 2.96: "And they followed the device which the devils devised against the kingdom of Solomon. And Solomon was not an unbeliever. But the devils believed not, they taught men sorcery and that which was sent down to the two angels at Babel, Harut and Marut. Yet those taught no man until they had said 'Verily, we are a temptation.'"

Zamakshari, 194 95; Text; Koran 2.96. 'And they followed the devices which the devils devised!' "They followed the book of Magic and of Witchcraft which they (the two angels) read." 'Against the kingdom of Solomon.' "Against the order of his kingdom and his land. And this the devils heard surreptitiously,[260] then they added falsehood to what they had heard and dictated it to the Kahims and they collected it in a book to read to and to teach man.

"And this spread in the land of Solomon of blessed memory so that they said that the Jinn knew the mysteries and that they called this the wisdom of Solomon, and the kingdom of Solomon was not perfect but by this knowledge and through it he subjugated men and Jinn."

[260] This is the story unencumbered by Zohra and other beauties.

'That which was sent down to the two angels at Babel, Harut and Marut.'

"It was the art of Magic, a trial from God for men. He who learns it from them and practises it is an unbeliever. And he who avoids it or learns it, not to practise it but to guard himself lest he become proud through it, he is a believer."

Geiger, *Was hat Mohammed* etc. 106, says: "The story because it deals with the Jinn and the angels seems to have been transferred by Mohammed to the time of Solomon." There was the more reason for it as Mohammed does not seem to have been plagued by chronological scruples whilst Bilkis, Ashmedai and their cycles all pointed to the time of Solomon.

(1) The Koran itself refers to sorcery only and not to any corruption of manners; immorality has been added by the commentators. (2) Harut and Marut—as far as the text of the Koran is concerned—may have come long before Solomon.

It is of value to be mindful of these things. ما يفرقون به بين المر وزوجه may well refer to black art and need not have any connection—in matter or tendency—with the Zohra episode.

Meshnevi (Jelalledin Rumi), p. 113: "A woman grown pale[261] because of an evil deed became the star of Zohra by transformation."

Hassan reads الملكين 'the two kings'—that they to whom the art of magic came down were two kings.[262]

[261] Grown yellow, i. e. ashamed. The Turkish Commentary tells us that Zuhra (= Anahid = Venus) had quarrelled with her husband and came to Harut and Marut for a judicial sentence. Harut and Marut had come to the earth to know the frailties of men. We get the same story, she asks them to commit the three sins of idolatry, murder (her own husband) and the drinking of wine. Then she will yield to their desire. They agree to drink wine, while refusing to do the rest. But Zohra asked of them the word by means of which, etc.
Mohammed (according to a Hadith) on seeing the Venus cursed her. 'God curse Zohra. She led two angels into temptation, Harut and Marut.'

[262] Here we have the Koran commented on without reference to Venus and all the embellishments of the story. Hassan's reading too is recorded, but without protest. Should we see in Zamakhshari a folklore purist?

APPENDICES

I

ADAM BEFORE THE FALL

(A) *In Jewish Lore*

According to Midrash Genesis Rabba 14, the dust out of which Adam was formed was taken from the place on which the altar stood. Jerusalem was supposed to be the central point of the Earth, so that Adam was formed of the doubly prominent dust. (L. Ginsberg, Haggada bei den Kirchenvaetern).

Babli Ḥulin, 60a. "Adam was very tall, of extraordinary dimensions, of great beauty." But then all creatures—in their original form—were perfect. And 'that Adam, when created, was like a man of twenty' is due to other reasons besides the imagination and the desire to let God's Creation 'with his own hands' appear as grand as possible (ibid).

Gen. Rabba 17. "His wisdom surpasses that of the angels (in as far as knowledge of the names of all beasts is concerned). He was a prophet" (תרדמה meaning the prophetical ecstasy, LXX: ἔκστασις). But with all this there is nothing divine in Adam. There is superhuman splendor but it is clearly pointed out that Adam was not even "holy".

Babli ʿErubin 18b. R. Meir said: "Adam was a truly pious man; when he saw that he had been punished with death, he fasted for 130 years, separated himself from his wives for 130 years and for the same period he put on garments of fig leaves".

Gen. Rabba 20. R. Jeremiah ben Eleazar said: "All the years that Adam lived in banishment he begat spirits, demons and night demons, for it is said 'Adam lived 130 years and (then) he begat (children) in his image, according to his likeness (Gen. 5, 3)'. Hence we can infer that before that time he begat creatures neither of his image nor of his likeness."

Bab. Pesaḥim 54a. R. Jehuda b. Menassiah said: "The splendor of Adam's heel obscured the sun. God made Adam for Himself, the sun for Adam. It is obvious that what He made for Himself would be more glorious than what He made for Adam."

(B) *In Christian Lore*

"Adam was formed out of the dust of the place where he lies buried. It is Golgotha where Jesus was crucified." This is a logical development of the central idea. To the Jewish mind nothing could be holier than the place on which the Altar stood, whilst the place of the Cross occupied a similar position in Christian lore. Ginsberg, *l. c.* p. 28, where see also for later developments p. 7.

The statement of Epiphanius that according to Jewish authorities Adam is buried in Golgotha, appears unjustified. The Talmud, Midrash and Hieronymus mention Hebron as Adam's last habitation.

Schatzhoehle ch. 3: 'And Adam extended himself and stood in the middle of the earth where the cross of the Messiah was put up, for in Jerusalem was Adam created.'

The main difference between the Jewish and the Christian legend of Adam lies in the fact that the latter was stimulated by the tendency to identify Adam in all his characteristics with Jesus, who similarly is represented as the 'Perfect

Man.' The 'twenty' years of rabbinic tradition become 'thirty', the age of Jesus at his death.

II

Consequences of the Fall

(A) Jewish

Gen. Rabba 17, commenting on Joshua 17, 15. 'The greatest among the Anakim.' R. Levi said: "Adam here stands for Abraham, and he was called Adam because he deserved to have been created before Adam. But the Holy One, blessed be He, said: 'Peradventure he may do wrong and there will be none to redress it, I shall therefore create Adam first so that in case he do wrong Abraham might come and make up for it.' *Babli Shabbat 55a,* '*Arakin 17a.* There is no death without sin! If the Holy One, blessed be He, had judged Abraham, Isaac and Jacob according to the strict law (without mercy) they would have been unable to stand the trial."

What do these passages teach us with regard to man and sin?—Above all that no human being is perfect. The Torah has taught the same. Moses, than who no man was greater, sinned; Jacob, David, Solomon sinned. Not because of any original sin in them which kept them away from the path of life, but because of man's weakness. Their life, in spite of their sins, is exemplary, the prophets refer to them as models to be imitated, yet they were mere men and thus not infallible. Later on reverent tradition wove a halo round their heads, but the Torah was emphatic enough, telling us that Moses and David, like Jacob, all lived a high life and yet sinned. It is this tradition which rabbinic literature carries on. It is important to compare this with the Christian view of original sin which is of quite a different nature. The writings of the various Christian Fathers make that abundantly clear.[263]

Adam sinned and through his sin brought death into the world. The Yezer Hara' must have been in him before he sinned; for he could not have disobeyed God, if the Yezer had not urged him. The evil inclination is a corollary of the freedom of the will, which Adam possessed; the angels do not sin, because they have no freedom of will. What Adam through his transgression introduced to man, then, was not the evil desire, but death. Man is perfectly free to choose, the power for good in him is not inferior to the forces for evil, it is his sovereign self which decides and not some irresistible corruptive energy which, in spite of himself, carries him headlong into the abyss of damnation. That is the Jewish view. There is only one sin: that of Adam, with but one consequence: death. The Christian Fathers know of a double sin: the disobedience of Adam and the infection of the lustful angels of Genesis 6, 4. Samael, according to Jewish lore, infected man with lasciviousness, of which Sinai purged Israel, obedience to God's Law removing lasciviousness from those who might otherwise be affected by its temptations. Satan and the Angels, according to Christian lore, hopelessly corrupted man, whose restoration is impossible before God's Redemption. Life is vitiated, no uplifting is feasible, all is darkness and corruption.

Babli Aboda Zara, 8a. "Adam is truly repentant. When Friday draws to its end and darkness covers the whole earth—a thing unexpected by him, for he knew nothing of the course of nature—he attributes it all to his own guilt and laments his sin. When the sun rises on the first Saturday, he is full of gratitude. The angels come down with

---
[263] See sub (B). "In the Fathers of the Church".

musical instruments and sing his psalm of the Sabbath day" ('Erubin, 18b). All is forgiveness and happiness.

Pirke d. R. Eliezer, 11.—A later development.—"Adam on the first day of the week went into the waters of the upper Giḥon until the waters reached up to his neck and he fasted seven weeks of days...until his body became like a species of seaweed.

Adam said before the Holy One, blessed be He: 'Sovereign of all worlds! Remove, I pray Thee, my sins from me and accept my repentance, and all the generations will learn that repentance is a reality!'—What did the Holy One, blessed be He, do? He put forth His right hand and accepted his repentance and took away from him his sin, as it is said: 'I acknowledge my sin unto Thee and mine iniquity have I not hid' (Ps. 59.3). I said I will confess my transgression unto the Lord, and Thou forgavest the iniquity of my sin. Selah. 'Selah in this world and Selah in the world to come.—'"

The result of his repentance is his re-admission, after death, into Paradise. Nothing remains of the consequences but death, man being mortal (Gen. Rabba 21, 23).

(B) In the Fathers of the Church

We have seen that in rabbinic literature the curse of man meant that he was deprived of the happy innocence of the life in Paradise, that he would have to eat his bread by the sweat of his brow, that Eve would suffer the pains of conception and pregnancy.

Embellishments: that man lost his original beauty, physical strength and greatness.

The result of Samael's lying with Eve was his infecting her with lasciviousness, of which Sinai cured all who stood at its foot to receive the Law. This infection with sensual passion was the only thing which remained for a time as the result of the Fall. Sinai having healed it, life goes on happily, there is no conception of innate misery and wretchedness. The Yezer Hara' is not in itself bad, it is on the one hand the necessary condition for freedom of will, on the other hand it is made useful in that it helps to propagate the human species, it stimulates study (the ambition of the disciples to surpass each other).[264] Man is quite capable of working out his own salvation both here and there by his own free choice to do good. He is in need of no mediator. The practical ethics of daily life therefore are the only things he has to care about. 'Not the study but the deed is the main thing (Pirke Abot).' The curse, except for the loss of Paradise and the necessity for hard work and the pains of childbearing, is practically non-existent.

The New Testament and the Christian Fathers.

The following quotations may help to illustrate their view: *Enchiridion, 48.* "That one sin, however, which was so great and committed in a place and state of so great happiness that in one man, by way of origin, and so to say, by way of root, the whole human race was condemned."—

And if the question arises: Why that? Why this exaggeration of Adam's sin and the punishment resulting from it, of which Jewish sources speak so differently? The answer is supplied by the second part of the same paragraph.

Ibid.: "It is not loosed and washed away, but only through one Mediator between God and Man, the man Jesus Christ, who alone could be so born that to him there was no need to be born again."

Ibid. 51: "Whence the Apostle says (Rom. V. 16–18): 'Not as by one man sinning, so is the gift also: for the judgment indeed was one unto condemnation but the grace of many offences unto justification.' Because assuredly that

---

[264] See Babli Aboda Z. l. c., also Erubin 18b.

one sin which is derived by way of descent, even if it be alone, makes men liable to condemnation: but the grace justifies from many offences the man who besides that one which in common with all he hath derived by way of descent, hath added many of his own likewise.

"As by the offence of one upon all men unto condemnation so also by the righteousness of one upon all men unto justification of life sufficiently shows that no one born of Adam is otherwise than held under condemnation, and that no one is freed from condemnation otherwise than by being born again in Christ."

According to the Talmud (Babli Shabbat 146a; Yeb. 103b) the curse of Eve's Fall was that the serpent infected her with lasciviousness. The lasciviousness in itself was the punishment.

Augustine takes it differently (Enchiridion, XXVI):
"Hence after his sin being made an exile, his own race also, which by sinning he had corrupted in himself as in its root, he bound by the punishment of death and condemnation. So that whatever progeny should be born of him and of his wife, through whom he had sinned, condemned together with him, *through carnal lust*, wherein was repaid a punishment similar to the disobedience, should draw along with it original sin, whereby it should be drawn, through various errors and pains, to the last never ending punishment with the apostate angels, its corruptions, masters and partners."

Whence has Augustine the apostate angels, the corruptors, masters and partners? One should assume he is referring to the cycles of legends which clustered round Gen. 6, 4. But then he rejects the interpretation of Bene Elohim= angels.

Further: The sin originally committed was due to

disobedience, not to carnal lust. 'Carnal lust' does not mean the weakness of the human heart, because Augustine expressly refers to angels as corruptors, masters and partners.

Moralia. VIII, 31. "It is through ourselves that we have been brought to the ground, but *to rise again by our own strength is beyond our ability.*"

Ibid. 32. "Being taken captive by the persuasions of the Serpent he became the enemy of Him whose precepts he despised."

Ibid. XI, 68. "By the weight of its changeableness the mind is always driven forward to some thing of a nature different from its own and, except it be kept in its stay by stringent discipline in self keeping, it is always sliding back into worse. For that mind which deserted Him, who ever standeth, lost the stay in which she might have continued."

Ibid. XXIV. "Man's righteousness will be restored to him by God's redemption!"

Ibid. XXII, 15. "If no decay of sin had ever ruined our first parent, he would not have begotten himself children of hell[265] but they all, who must now be saved by the Redemption, would have been born of his elect soul."[266]

---

[265] Ibidem, Chapter 32. 'But whosoever are not through the one Mediator between God and man set free from that mass of perdition which was caused through the first man, they too themselves also will rise again each with his own flesh, but only that they may be punished together with the devil and his angels.'—*The Fall of the Angels is here seen to be of greatest consequence* in Gregory's theology.

[266] There are three Adam traditions:
  I. Satan hates him, hence seduction. Esp. Koran, Schatzhoehle.
     envies him, hence seduction, Gen. Rabba, Aboth d. R. Nathan.
  II. Adam glorious
     Angels want to say 'holy', God restrains them—Talmud.
     God commands them to worship Adam—Christian.
  III. Adam modest
     All angels call him 'Lord', but he shows that only God deserves this title.
     P. d. R. E. XI., Tanh. Pek. 3.

III.

Other Falls of Satan

Abot de R. Nathan, ed. Schechter p. 164: "Satan went and said before the Holy One, blessed be He: 'Lord of the Universe! I have gone to and fro in the whole earth and I did not find a man loving[267] Thee except Job. Thou hast testified concerning him three times: 'He was perfect, upright, fearing God and averse to evil.' Now, give me permission (to do so) and I'll turn his heart from Thee.' And the Holy One, blessed be He said to him: 'Satan, Satan, what have you to do[268] with my servant Job, for there is none like him in the whole earth?' Satan replied: 'O Lord of the Universe! Give me permission and I shall turn his heart from Thee.' Then the Holy One, blessed be He replied: 'Behold, all his possessions are in thy hand.' Satan went disguised as Job himself[269] and led into captivity his flock, cattle, camels, smiting the herds, and the shepherds. A fugitive came to tell (Job about it). He said to him: 'The oxen were ploughing and the she-asses feeding beside them, etc.'—Job at once[270] opened his mouth and said: 'The Lord has given, the Lord has taken, blessed be the name of the Lord.' Satan went again and found Job's sons and daughters eating and drinking wine in the house of their eldest brother. The firstborn was lying on the roof, when Satan threw him upon them, thereby killing them all.[271] A fugitive

---

[267] Lit.: 'I have not found a man loving before Thee except Job.' 'Before Thee' is reminiscent of the Targum, cp. Onkelos, Numbers 22, 9, 13, 20.

[268] מלך "What is to thee, what can you expect to achieve with Job, seeing that he is perfect in devotion?"

[269] Why that? The Sabean invaders are sufficient cause of loss. Probably this is meant to indicate that all misfortune that befell Job was due to Satan's personal activity. The Sabeans may have attacked his shepherds for a private vendetta or any other reason. Satan afflicted him for his Satanic purpose.

[270] The Agadic "immediately".

[271] see sub (269).

came to tell Job,[272] saying: 'Thy sons and daughters were eating and drinking wine in the house of their eldest brother and behold a wind, etc.' Job opened his mouth and said: 'The Lord has given, etc.' Satan returned (from afflicting Job) and stood before the Holy One, blessed be He, and said before Him: 'Lord of the Universe, I have gone to and fro in the whole earth and I have found none loving[273] Thee except Job.'

"And the Holy One, blessed be He said: 'Hast thou considered my servant Job?' Satan answered: 'Skin for Skin, etc. But now give me permission to afflict himself (his body).' The Holy One, blessed be He replied: 'Behold he is in thy hand, but guard his life (only spare his life).' He replied: 'Lord of the Universe! This resembles the case of a mortal king who said to his servant: "Go forth and break the barrel but keep the wine; how am I to spare his life? (whilst afflicting him most grievously to tempt him to transgress.)"'

"The Holy One, blessed be He said: 'I have told you already,[274] spare his life (otherwise you may afflict him as much as you like).' Satan immediately went down with great joy and smote him with sore boils.

"And Job took him a potsherd to scrape himself withal. His wife said to him: 'Art thou still holding fast thine integrity? etc.' Job rebuked her and told her: 'Thou speakest as one of the impious women speak.' When he had made the house evil smelling for him, he went and sat on the dunghill until his flesh stank. And worms came down from him and they made his whole body into holes, so that one group quarreled with the other. What did Job do? He took one of the worms and put it on its hole,

[272] כפלים is probably a misreading for הפליט, or it should mean that Satan himself came to Job in the disguise of a refugee, to see and hear of his apostasy as a result of the calamities that had befallen him.
[273] אהוב mistake for אוהב, the pass. part. giving no sense.
[274] Reading כבר for הכבד.

and another one (or, the other one of the quarrelling parties), putting it on its hole, and said to them: 'That is my flesh, why should you quarrel about it?' And his heart was grieved within him. Then he said to the Holy One, blessed be He: 'Lord of the Universe! There is no mediator between us (better: Is there any, etc.). Let him put his hand (exercise his power) over us two. Let him put his rod away from me and let not his truth terrify me.' He gave thanks and praise to God, for all his qualities (Mercy and Justice, cp. מדת הדין ומדת הרחמים) and concerning him it is said: 'I gave thanks to Thee that Thou wert angry at me, may Thy anger turn, and mayest Thou comfort me.' At that hour all the inhabitants of the world believed in him, that there was none like him in the whole earth. Thereupon the Holy One, blessed be He, said to Satan: 'Satan! Satan! Didst thou not say thus: "Give me permission (to afflict him) and I will cause his heart to turn?"' Immediately God rebuked Satan most vehemently, as it is said: 'And the Lord said unto Satan, "The Lord rebuke thee O Satan!"' He rebuked him and threw him down from heaven, as it is said: 'Truly like (ordinary) men shall ye die and like one of the Princes shall ye fall!' This sentence refers to Satan whom God had cast down from heaven".[275]

The Apocalypse of Sedrach: Menzies, Ante-Nicene Christian Library, Addit. Vol. p. 177. "And Sedrach saith to him:[276] 'Of Thy will Adam was beguiled, my Lord. Thou didst command Thine angels to make approach to Adam and the first of the Angels himself transgressed Thy commandment and did not make approach to him. And Thou didst

---

[275] Isaiah 14, 12 combined with Zech. 3, 1 f.—Yet this is no rebellious Lucifer.—

[276] This is a curious story. According to it we must assume that God sent an angel to tempt Adam; that Angel would not go and for this disobedience was banished. There is no indication in rabbinic lore of anything like this. This account excludes all stories about Satan's (or Samael's or the Devil's) Fall from heaven because of his having seduced Adam to eat from the forbidden fruit, against the express prohibition of God.

banish him, because he transgressed Thy commandment and did not make any approach to the work of Thine hands.'"

The Devil fighting God. Sedrach, vide Menzies, Ante-Nicene Library Addit. Vol. p. 177. "Why didst thou not slay the Devil, the worker of unrighteousness? Who is able to fight an invisible spirit? And he as a smoke enters into the hearts of men and teaches them every sin.—He fights against Thee, the immortal God, and what can wretched man then do to him?"

IV.

Other "Fallen Angels"

Gen. Rabba 50. Text Gen. 19. 13. 'For we are going to destroy this place'. (The angels ask Lot to take his relatives and flee from the doomed city). R. Levi in the name of R. Samuel:[277] "Because the ministering angels betrayed the mysteries of the Holy One, blessed be He, they were driven from their department for a hundred and thirty eight years".[278] R. Tanḥuma made the charge easier.[279] R. Ḥama b. Ḥanina said: "(They were expelled)[280] because they behaved arrogantly in saying: 'We are going to destroy this place.'"[281]

Gen. Rabba 68. 'Ascending and descending on the ladder'. "The angels who had to descend from their sphere to dwell outside it for 138 years, now descended. That is the reason why the Bible says 'Ascending and descending';

---

[277] God had not made it known even to Abraham.

[278] According to the Sefer Yezirah this was the time between their coming to Lot and ascending again in Jacob's dream. Cp. Abr. b. David a. l. and Rabbi Bachya b. Asher to Genesis 28, 12.

[279] Not implying betrayal or secret, but loose talk, agreeing probably with what ben Hanina says.

[280] An indication of this (if any) fall is seen by some Rabbi in 'Lo, the Erelim cry outside (Isaiah 33.7)' i. e. outside their sphere, they must have been ousted then.

[281] They were only messengers of God. It was God, not they, who wrought the destruction.

one should have expected angels to descend first, then to ascend again. But the angels referred to here are those who had been in ill grace owing to having betrayed God's secret, or having talked arrogantly."

V.

The Nine and Ten Orders

Gregory, Homilia, 34: "We know on the authority of Scripture that there are nine orders of angels, viz: Angels, Archangels, Virtues, Powers, Principalities, Dominions, Thrones, Cherubim and Seraphim. St. Paul, too, writing to the Ephesians, enumerates four orders, when he says 'Above all Principality and Power and Virtue and Dominion.' And again writing to the Colossians, he says: 'Whether Thrones or Dominions, or Principalities or Powers.' If we now join these two lists together we have five orders, and adding Angels, Archangels, Cherubim and Seraphim, we find nine orders of angels."

Now the ten orders of Aelfric, reduced by one through the fall of Lucifer and his troop, are to be replenished through man. Gregory has nine without any mention of the loss. (Compare the enumeration in the Passover Agada. It is a most remarkable parallel). Once the nine orders of angels had become a fact, sub-divisions became necessary. We have three such in Jewish and Christian lore. In the former much later, restricted to Cabbalistic literature, in Christian writings comparatively early.

Thomas Aquinas, Summa Theologiae, I, 108: 'There are three Hierarchies, each of which contains three orders.

(1) Seraphim, Cherubim, Thrones.
(2) Dominations, Virtues, Powers.
(3) Principalities, Archangels, Angels.'
Cp. S. Denis, De Coelesti Hierarchia.

The Jewish doctrine of the ten Sephirot is probably of Gnostic origin. The 'Intelligences' are ordinary Neoplatonism. The Cabbalists draw attention to the following 'Tens':

(A) Ten names of God in the Hebrew Bible. (B) Ten orders of Angels in the Hebrew Bible. (C) Three heavens and seven planets. (D) Ten members of the human body. (E) Ten Commandments.

Once 'ten' had an important meaning, the other 'tens' would follow through association of ideas. (Cp. M.H. Farbridge, Symbolism, 1924). Gregory, Moralia, XXXII, 47, following Ez. 28, 13: 'Every precious stone was thy covering, the sard, and topaz, and jasper, the chrysolite, the onyx, and the beryl, the sapphire, and carbuncle, and the emerald.' "He mentions nine kinds of stones, doubtless because there are nine orders of angels. For, when in the very words of Scripture, Angels, Archangels, Thrones, Dominations, Virtues, Princedoms, Powers, Cherubim and Seraphim are plainly spoken of and mentioned, it is shown how great are the distinctions of the citizens of heaven. And yet the Behemoth is decribed as being covered by them because he had those as a vesture for his adornment, by comparison with whom he was more brilliant when he transcended their brightness."

Behemoth in Job 40, 14 of course does not stand for Lucifer but Gregory explains it so. The nine stones of course mean anything but nine orders of angels, but such exegesis fits the then tendency. According to a timehallowed word 'one does not argue with an Agadist'—אין משיבין על הדרוש—for the idea is all he intends to convey, the text is just a peg to hang it on. (For a beautiful paraphrastic account of Lucifer's fall, with mystical details, see *Ibidem* 23, 48). In Moralia 32, 47 Gregory mentions nine orders of angels, all of which are covered by the tenth; the nine being the vesture, which is important only for what it contains. A striking parallel—though altogether different in import and tendency—is the relation of the nine Sephirot to the tenth, the En-Soph, which equally covers them all, and which equally bestows dignity upon them.

Once Lucifer is seen in the shining star of the morning, the adjective ornantia becomes obvious. It is remarkable however that in all these passages Gregory does not even once refer to Lucifer, seemingly accepting him as an entity independent of the text. Similarly does Rabbi Simeon ben Yohai reject the translation of Bene Elohim as Malakim (angels) (Gen. Rabba a. l.), and yet in the Zohar the story of fallen angels is told repeatedly and emphatically. And, to bring a later parallel, Rabbi Jacob Emden, in his Mitpahat Sepharim, reduces the Zohar to fragments, whilst in his interpretation of the Siddur he does not go one step without the Zohar. No doubt answers will be available to all these apparent inconsistencies. The most convenient one lies in the differentiation between פשט (the plain simple meaning of the text) and דרש (homiletical interpretation).

Ten orders in the Talmud. (though not of angels). Babli Hagiga, 12a: 'By means of ten things the world was created: Wisdom, Insight, Knowledge, Force, Power, Severity, Justice, Right, Love and Mercy.'

'Ten things were created on the first day. They are: Heaven, Earth, Tohu, Bohu, Light, Darkness, Day, Night, Wind and Water.'

See *W. Bacher*, Die Agada der babyl. Amoräer, 20f.

VI.

Azazel

(1) Gesenius takes it to be equal to עֲזֵלְזֵל, a strengthened form of עזל = 'to remove', here 'complete removal', perdition personified, like Sheol and Abaddon.—D. Hoffman, Lev. I, 444: "Die ganze Gemeinde soll sich zuerst als 'Sair' Gott weihen, dann wird der andere Sair alle Seienden der gaenzlichen Vernichtung preisgeben."

(2) LXX: ἀποπομπαῖος, Symm.: ἀπολελυμένος agree in main with Gesenius. Yet both, at first sight, present a difficulty. For, if Azazel means 'ἀποπομπαῖος' ("one to be sent away"), then verse 10 'to send him to the wilderness' seems superfluous. It is not too difficult to overcome this exegetically. For our present purpose it is more helpful to point out that LXX and Symm. insist on 'ἀποπομπαῖος' and 'ἀπολελυμένος' respectively, as they are eager to hand on the genuine Jewish tradition which they had received; the more so since the Aza and Azael legends threatened to swamp it.—There is no prototype of Azazel in Babylonian lore (K. A. T. 3).

Levit. 17, 17 forbids any sacrifice to demons. Only late literature (like P. d. R. E.) is influenced by the invasion of demons from Persia. The goat of Azazel is sent off and killed. Both goats have one and the same purpose, to obtain God's forgiveness. No cult of Azazel is mentioned. Ἀποπομπαῖος is the main idea.

Reasons for Azazel—ἀποπομπαῖος

(1) Already in LXX taken as such.
(2) It is not sacrificed, nor offered, but sent to take away the sins. Cp. its name 'Sair Hamishtaleah', שעיר המשתלח.

(3) It is parallel to Levit 14, 7, where the bird equally takes away impurity.

(4) The interpretation of Tanna de be Eliyahu does not refer to Satan at all, it 'explains' the name of the mountain.

(5) No connection with Satan occurs before P. d. R. E.

(6) P. d. R. E. disagrees with Talm. Bab. Yoma 29a, Lev. Rabba 21.

(7) 'Erez Gezerah' indicates destruction.

MY OWN EXPLANATION OF AZAZEL

עז אזל = The cruel, rough Azel. This may have been the original meaning, before the fallen angels were brought into contact with it, changing the rock into a demon. Azel as a rock occurs in I Sam. 20, 19. With this would agree (a) Yoma 67b: The Rabbis taught (the *official* view as against the individual ones which follow) Azazel: "That is the name of a rough and rocky mountain."

(b) The Mishna Yoma VI, 6 gives the following account of what happened with the he-goat, sent to Azazel: "He divided the crimson colored strap, one half being bound to the rock and the other half between his two horns, and he thrust him backwards. The goat was hurled down and rolling was reduced to fragments before reaching one half of the mountain."—(Cp. also note 197).

Babli Yoma 67b:—After the official explanation of Azazel, the one which lived as the right one in the consciousness alike of priest, teacher and layman, the Talmud in its usual broadness of mind gives access to the play of folklore.

VII.

The Agada of the Christian Fathers

(a) Al Tikre אל תקרי.

This method is only possible with the original Hebrew text. The author desires to give the text a somewhat different meaning and since in its present form it does not embody what he intends to say, he proposes ad hoc a slight emendation. The text now makes it clear what the Agadist wishes to convey. (Cp. the introduction p. 2).

The Fathers of the Church use only translations, at any rate for their discourses. It is but rarely that an argument or theory is based upon, or derived from, a peculiarity or a minutia of the original Hebrew. Consequently a strict Al Tikre is impossible. The step nearest to it would be to give any passage a meaning that will not be too improbable in the wording of the sentence, a sort of Al Tikre with limitations. This approach to Al Tikre exists. In the 3rd chapter of the 4th book of his Moralia on Job, Gregory the Great speaks of the Apostate Angel, connecting it somehow or other with the 4th verse of Chapter IV.

"Forasmuch then, as mankind is brought to the light of Repentance by the coming of the Redeemer, but the Apostate Angel is not recalled by any hope of pardon, or with any commendment of conversion, to the light of a restored estate, it may well be said: 'Let not God regard it from above neither let the light shine upon it!' *As though it were plainly expressed*:

"For that he hath himself brought on the darkness—let him bear without end what himself has made, nor let him ever recover the light of his former condition, since he parted with it even without being persuaded thereto."

For further references cp. Book V. ch. 2.

(b) אין ... אלא 'En Ella.

The Jewish Agadists when, for the moment, they identify very different things, use the phrase:—אין ... אלא 'X is nothing but Y.' E. g. "The Torah is compared to *water*, for in Deut. 32, 1 it reads:—'My speech shall flow like dew, like showers.'" The Agadist on some occasion will now make use of that passage to say אין מים אלא תורה "Water cannot mean anything but Torah." —Cp. Hagigah 12a: "And good cannot refer to anything but the righteous." Exactly the same phrase is used by Gregory on Ezekiel 31, 8, 9, where he appropriated for Behemoth a passage referring to Babylon. 'The Cedars in the Paradise of God were not higher, the fir trees equalled not his summit, the plane trees were not equal to his branches, nor any tree in the Paradise of God was like his and his beauty, etc.' Now says Gregory, *Moralia 32, 23:* '*Who can be understood by Cedars, Fir trees, etc. unless heavenly virtues?*'

Moralia IV, 12. Text Job 3, 6. 'Let it not be joined unto the days of the year.'—"*Now what is meant by* 'the days', but the several minds of the elect?"

Gregory, Book IV, 15.—Text Job, 3, 3. 'Let them curse it that curse the *day*.' i. e. let those elect spirits by condemning denounce the darkness of his erring ways, who see the *grandeur of his shining array* from the first a deceit.[282]

Moralia 38, 15. Text Job 38, 15. 'And the high arm shall be broken'. "For *what else is the 'high arm' to be taken*, but the proud loftiness of the Antichrist?"

[282] Similarly are יום 'day' and לילה 'night' taken as symbols of prosperity and misfortune, grandeur and misery respectively, in rabbinic Agada.

Ibid 29, 13. *Text: Ps. 89,9.* 'O Lord, who is like unto Thee' used for man's repentance as the Agadists use any passage for any end.

Ibid 29.20. 'Hast thou held and shaken the ends of the earth and hast thou shaken the wicked out of it.' "By 'earth' is designated man of whom it was said,—Gen. 3, 19—'Earth thou art, to Earth shalt thou go.'"

(c) הצד השוה. 'Common Traits'. (cp. Babli Baba Mezia, 5a).

Gregory, Book IV, 2. Text: Job, 3, 6. 'Let it not be joined unto the days of the year. Let it not come in the number of the months.' "By a year we may understand the multitude of the redeemed. For as the year is produced by a number of days, so by the assemblage of all the righteous there results that countless sum of the elect." That is indeed an extreme case, probably without any parallel.

(d) An interesting and very bad case of Agadic etymology:

'Satanas'.—'Sata' in the Jewish and Syrian language means apostate, and 'nas' is the word from which serpent is derived; from both of which is formed Satanas. See note 70.

With these considerations in view, books ascribed to Jews because of their Agadic form, would now need other evidence for their Jewish origin to be established.

VIII.

1. Augustine on the Theory of Substitution (Ersatz Theorie)

Enchiridion XXIX. "It therefore pleased God, the Creator and Governor of the Universe, that, seeing that not the whole multitude of angels had perished by deserting

God, the part which had perished should remain in eternal perdition; whilst the part which had continued firm with God, when the others forsook him, should rejoice in the full and certain knowledge of the Eternity of its future happiness. But that, in that the other rational creature which was in man had perished entire through sins and punishment both original and actual, out of the renewal of a part of it should be supplied whatever loss that fall of the devil had brought on the fellowship of the angels. For this has been promised to the Saints at their Resurrection that 'they shall be equal to the Angels of God.'"

Here then we have the nucleus of the 'Ersatztheorie' which is unknown to Jewish literature. Augustine was the teacher of Pope Gregory I, who developed this story in a somewhat different direction. Whilst according to Augustine the fellowship of the angels would remain diminished up to the time when the saints will be resurrected, Gregory tells us that it was in order to replace the fallen legions of the devil that man (Adam) was created. For details see the quotation from Aelfric's Homily appended below. It is not too difficult to account for this divergence of opinion.[283]

Once it was established that the order of the fallen angels was to be replaced by man—and such theories were taken to be the truth, the whole truth, and nothing but the truth—this could be and, as we see, was, applied wherever thought fit or necessary.

As to the origin of the 'Ersatztheorie'—whether it came from Augustine or from one of his teachers—I believe it is due to an Agadistic interpretation of the sentence (Luke XX, 26) which happened to strike the author in connection with the fall of Satan. The Church Fathers had many

---

[283] Cp. also Enoch ch. 62. 'From the very redemption of men the losses of the fall of angels are repaired.'

Jewish teachers who initiated them into the method of Agada. What is more natural than that their continued occupation with rabbinic lore should cause them to think and expound in a similar manner, divesting, for a moment, in pursuit of a definite idea, a sentence of its textual and contextual meaning and bestowing upon it an interpretation ad hoc quod erat demonstrandum?[284] It becomes very obvious that this is the case with Jerome who abounds in Agadisms of his own, and the present instance is just as good as any other. The passage in Luke, as it stands, refers to the blessedness of the Saints when, united with their Father in Heaven, in holiness and happiness, they shall be equal to the angels, yet the passage lends itself to the interpretation Augustine has put upon it.[285]

IX.

AN EDITION OF AELFRIC 1623, WHICH MILTON MAY HAVE USED. B.M.C. 65 I.1.

The Almighty Creator, when He created the angels, in His wisdom made ten[286] armies of them on the first day.[287] And the angels dwelt in Glory with God. Within six days after the true God had created the world[288] as He had meant to create it, one of the angels, very prominent among the others, considered how beautiful he was, and how splendid in glory, and he understood his strength, how mighty he had been created; his honor too pleased him greatly. Lucifer he was called, that means 'Bearer of the Light', because of the exceptional brightness of his glorious face. And he considered it humiliating for him—eminent

---

[284] For the later development see Langland, Piers Plowman I, and Miss Smith's Edition of the York Plays.
[285] See Euchiridion XIV for a fine yet characteristically agadic interpretation of Isaiah 5, 20.
[286] See Sub "9 and 10 Orders". Aelfric uses Gregory I.
[287] See Note on 'The Creation of the Angels' p. 15.
[288] There is a contradiction between this and the statement that six days after this affair, God made Adam. The theory of substitution is hinted at or implied.

as he was—to obey any master, and refused to worship his Creator and to thank Him duly for what he had received whereas, especially for the glory bestowed upon him, he ought to have subjected himself.

But he would not have his Maker to lord over him, nor continue in the truth of the Son of God who made him so fair, but he schemed by treason to attain the Kingdom and to make himself God.

So great was his arrogance.

And he collected about him very zealously bands to conspire with him in his impious striving.—But he found no seat to sit upon, for no part of Heaven would bear him nor could there be any kingdom against the will of God, who made all. Then the proud one saw what his might was, for he had no place to rest upon[289] but fell, changed into a devil[290] with all his companions, from the Court of the Lord to the torments of Hell, as he deserved it.

Six days after this had happened[291] Almighty God created Adam from the Earth with His own hands and gave him a soul; and soon afterwards He made Eve out of a rib of Adam that they and their posterity might enjoy that fair estate which the Devil forfeited, if they remain obedient to their Maker.

Hence the Devil soon afterwards seduced them, so that they broke (the Covenant) and transgressed the Command of God, very speedily. Thus both became subject to death[292] and were driven from that joy down to the earth.

This is the type of the complete story before Milton. The notes give short references to the chapters, which deal with the point in question, drawing attention to modifications.

[289] Cp. Piers Plowman I.
[290] Isaiah 14, Hades taken as abode of the devil. See sub Lucifer. In the Koran "a stoned devil".
[291] This is the implication of the theory of substitution.
[292] Cp. chapter IV, sub 'The Oath of Revenge'.

LITERATURE

(a) Texts:

Hebrew and Aramaic.

The Hebrew Bible, The Samaritan Pentateuch.
Midrashim: M. Rabba, 1545 Venice; ed. Theodor Berlin 1893, M. Aggada, Vienna 1894, M. Haggadol, Yalkut Hadash, Yalkut Reubeni, Yalkut Simeon Wilna 1898, M. Tanhuma, Wilna 1885, M. R. Rabbeti, M. Abkir, Vienna 1883.
Talmud: Babli, 1876, Warsaw, Yerushalmi, 1866 Krotoshin.
Abot de R. Natan ed. Schechter 1877, London.
Pirke de R. Eliezer, 1852, Warsaw.
Targum Onkelos ed. Berliner, 1884, Berlin.
The Samaritan Targum (Genesis) London n.d.
Targum Pseudo-Jonathan ed. Ginsburger, 1903, Berlin.
Tobit (Neubauer's edition), 1878, Oxford.
Eldad ha-Dani, ed. Epstein, 1891 Vienna.
Zohar 1558, Mantua.
Sefer Yezirah, 1562 Mantua.
  Bachya (Genesis), Venice 1566.
  Nachmanides, Wilna 1899.
  Recanati (Leviticus) Venice 1523.

Arabic.

Koran ed. Fluegel Leipzig 1836.
Tabari, Commentary, Beyrout, n.d.
Tabari History, ed. de Goeje 1879–1901, Leyden.
Zamakhshari, Kashaf ed. Meynard, 1876, Paris.
Kazwini, Cosmology, ed. Wuestenfeld.
El Balkhi, ed. Huart 1899–1907, Paris.

Syriac.

Bar Hebraeus, Chronicle ed. Bedjan, 1890 Paris.
Isaac of Antoich (ed. Bedjan) Homilies, Paris 1905.
Schatzhoehle, ed. Betzold, Leipzig 1912.

Persian.

Meshnevi, also ed. G. Rosen, 1913, Leipzig.

Greek.

LXX.

New Testament.
Philo, De Gigantibus.
Josephus, Antiquitates, ed. Niese, 1889–95 Leipzig.

Latin.

The Vulgate.
The Christian Fathers.

Anglo-Saxon.

Aelfric. Homilies.—De Initio Creaturae. 1623 London.
Beowulf. ed Heyne 1879, Paderborn.

English.

The York plays, ed. Smith (see ten Brink, Engl. Literatur I, 267).
Langland, Piers Plowman, London 1867 ed. W. Skeat.
Milton, Paradise Lost.

(b) General:

Gruenbaum, M., Gesammelte Aufsaetze, ed. F. Perles 1912.
Ginzberg, L., Die Haggada bei den Kirchenvaetern, Amsterdam 1899.
Roskoff M., Geschichte des Teufels 1869, Leipzig.
Schrader, E., K.A.T. 3rd Edit.
Jewish Encyclopedia.
Charles, R. H., Apocrypha, 2nd Vol. 1913.
Ante-Nicene Library.
Kennedy, Philo's Contribution to Religion 1919, London.
Schuerer, E., Geschichte, 3rd Ed. 1901–3 Leipzig.
Reitzenstein, R., Poimander, 1904 Leipzig.
—Mysterienreligionen, 1920 Leipzig 2nd ed.
Sale's edition of the Koran.
Schwab, M., Vocabulaire d' Angelologie.
Kohut, M., Juedische Angelologie, 1866 Leipzig.

Martini, R., Pugio Fidei 1651 Paris.
Epstein, A., in Magazin 1888–9; "R. Moses Hadarshan," 1891, Vienna.
Sprenger, A., Mohammad, 1869 Berlin.
Driver, S. R., The Ideals of the Prophets, 1915.
Dionysius, Areopagita, ed. Engelhardt, 1823.
Hoffman, D., Leviticus, 1905.
Delitzsch Franz, Isaiah, 1889.
Wohlgemuth J., Das Juedische Religionsgesetz, 1913–15.
Journal Asiatique, 1913.
The Hibbert Journal, 1902.
P. Lagarde, Gesammelte Abhandlungen, 1866.
Zunz, L., Gottesdienstliche Vortraege, 2d ed. 1892, Berlin.
Bousset, W., Religion des Judentums, 1903 Berlin.
—In Goettinger Gelehrte Anzeien, 1905.
Jeremias, A., Das alte Testament im Lichte des alten Orients, 3rd Edit.
Bacher, Agada der Tannaiten (AT), 1884–90.
—Agada der Palaest. Amoraeer (APA), 1891–99.
—Agada der Babyl. Amoraeer (ABA). 1878.
—Prooemien. 1913.
—Terminologie, Leipzig 1899.
Jewish Quarterly Review.
Z. D. M. G.
Ehrlich, Randglossen, Berlin 1899.
Geiger, A., Was hat Mohammed, etc. 2nd ed. Leipzig 1902.
Oppert, Expedition de Mesopotamie.
The Observatory, 1918.
The Journal of Theological Studies.

INDEX

INDEX

Aboda Zara, 8a: Adam's repentance, 143; 20b: etymology of Samael, 80; 20b: virtuous Satan, 38; 27b: on demons, 32.

Abot V: on miracles, 77.

Abot de R. Nathan: fall of man, 72ff; seven heavens, 14; (ed. Schechter, 164): Satan's fall and Job, 148ff.

Abraham, Rabbi: introd. to Haggadah, 5.

Adam: before the fall, 140ff; in Chr. lore, 141; in Paradise, 56ff.

Aelfric (ed. 1623): prob. used by Milton, 161ff.

Aeshma: and Ashmedai, 81.

Akiba, Rabbi: Esther story, 2; on preexistence of angels, 49.

Al-Rabi, 345, 19: angels and woman, 137.

Al Tikre: among Chr. Fathers, 157.

Angels: created before world: cf. Numb. 11; Dan. 7. 10; Hag. 14b; Yalkut Hadash; Gen. 1.26, and Philo ad locum; Job 1.6; Dan. 4.14; Jubilees; et al., 15. in Bib. lit., 12; nature of, 12; post-Bib., 12.

Angramainyus, 40–41.

Anmael: betraying virgin, 92.

Apocalypse of Sedrach, p. 177: fall of Satan, 151.

Aquinas, Thomas, Summa Theologiae, I, 108: nine orders of angels, 153.

Arakin, 17: imperfect man, 142.

Ashmedai: 81; not inimical to man, 89.

Athenagoras, XXIV, Defence of Christians: fall of angels, 122, 124.

Augustine, De Civitate Dei, XV, 22–23: on Gen. 6. 1–4, 106ff; Enchiridion, XIV, XV, 19; XXVI, 48, 51: original sin-Adam, 145–7; XXVII, 20; XXIX: theory of substitution, 159ff; LXX, 22; 28: angels cast down, 53. Of Continence, VI: 20.

Azazel: 155ff; author's explan., 156; reasons given for, 155.

Baba Batra, 15a: Josh. author of last verses, Deut.; Job as myth 4–16a: the virtuous Satan, 38.

Bacher, W., Die Agada der babyl. Amoraer, 20f: on "tens," 154 Winter und Wünsche, II, 270, 335: 68.

Bath Kol, 29.

Bene Elohim: identity of, 97ff; in Jos., Philo, N. T., 98.

Benoth Haadam: identity of, 103ff

Beowulf 1: origin of evil spirits, 34.

Berakot, 25b: good angels, 13; 51: angel of death and R. Josh. b. Levi, 39; 64a: interpreting Is. 54.13:3.

Bevan, A. A.: 133–34.

Bewer, J: Lit. of the O. T., 28.

Book of the Creation and Hist. of Harut and Marut, 127.

Book of Wisdom, 2.13: 30; 2.24: serpent as evil principle, 24.

Bousset, Religion des Judentums, 6.

Büchler, A., Types of Jewish Palestinian piety, 39.

Canticles, 8.13; character of angels, 14.

Catholic Enc., 6, p. 1: on authority 7; p. 4: In consensus, 8.
Chr. Fathers: dogma, 7.
Chronicles I, 21.1: Satan provokes David, 26.
Clemens Alex.: fall of angels, 123.
Clement A., III 297, Recognitions: fall of lustful angels, 124.
Creation of man, objected to: Jewish sources, 45; Moh. sources, 52.
Crescas: on articles of faith, 7.

Daiva (Satan), 58.
De Lagarde, P., Ges. Abhandlungen: on Harut and Marut, 131ff.
Delitzsch, Isaiah, 305: 27; New Comm. on Gen., I, 232f: meaning of Nephilim, 106.
Deut., 10.12: interpreted, 3; 32.17: satyrs, 26.
Dikduke Soferim: on Ketubot, 77a, 39.
Disputed passages: fallen angels in Bib., 17.
Driver, Ideals of the Prophets, 28.

Ecclesiastes, 2.8: interpretation, 83ff.
Eisenmenger: on Jewish lore, 6.
Emden, R. Jacob: on Zohar, 154.
En Ella: in Agada, 158.
Enoch, 6. 1ff, 7, 8.3, 10, 64: angels and women, 93ff; 13.5; 14.5; 64.4, 6: on Satan, 30.
Ephraem, 46.4: angels not sons of God, 121; 50.4: Satan's envy, 43; XXXVIII, 3: 43.
Epstein: R. Moses Hadarshan, 68, Eldad ha-Dani, 17.
Erubin, 18b: piety of Adam, 140.
Ersatztheorie, 160ff.
Esther Rabba 1: R. Akiba's interpretation, 2.
Esther, Targum Sheni: on Is. 14.12: 29.
(Midrash) Exodus Rabba, 15.7: on Is. 14.12: 29; 18.1: Samael as accuser, 79; 18.7: on Is. 14.12: 29.

Fall, the: consequences, 142ff.
Fall of angels, 90; causes, 121.
Fall of man, 68ff, 72ff.
Fallen angels, additional, 151.
Father, as title: authority, 7.
Fathers of church: agreement, 8.
Fisher, G. P., Hist. of Chr. Doctrine, 41f: non-Cath. views of Chr. authority, 9.
Freudenthal: Die Flavius Jos. zugeschr. Schrift, 31.

Geiger, Was hat Mohammed, 66, 139.
Genesis, 3.1ff: serpent, 14.
(Midrash) Genesis Rabba, 8.5: on Shemhazai and Azael, 104; 8.5: R. Simon on creation of man, 45; 8.10: R. Hosea on fall of Adam, 56; 9: Satan messenger of God, 37; 14: formation of Adam, 140; 17: on Joshua 17.15: 142; 17: wisdom of Adam, 140; 17.5: creation of man, 46; 18.2 on angels, 12; 19: punishment of serpent, 71; 19.4: slander of serpent, 70; 20: Adam begetter of spirits, 141; 20.4: punishment of serpent, 72; 26.2: R. Simon b. Yohai, on Bene Elohim, 116; 26.4: "Bene Elohim," 117; 26.4: names of Nephilim, 110; 48.11: good angels, 13; 50: on Gen. 19.13: fallen angels, 151; 56: the virtuous Satan, 36; 68: fallen angels, 151–2.
Gesenius: on Azazel, 155; on Nephilim, 106.
Ginzberg, L.: Adam in Jewish Lore, 140.
Gittin, 68a: faults of Ashmedai, 82; 68ff: the virtuous Satan, 38.
Goldziher: Muhammed und Islam, 19–11.

Gregorius Nyssenus: on Creation, 49.
Gregory, Homilia, 34: nine and ten orders of angels, 152; Moralia, preface, 8: God and Devil, 43; 2.38; 18.71; 27.66: Jewish angel tradition, 19; 11.4; Satan before God, 44; 29.13 on Ps. 89.9; 29.20 on Gen. 3.19; 38.15 on Job 38.15: En Ella, 158; II, 3: on virtue of angels, 23; II, 20: on IKings, 22, 19ff, 22 IV, 2: on Job 3.6-'Haṣad Hashaveh,' 159; IV, 12: on Job, 3.6-En Ella, 157; IV, 15: on Job, 3.3: 158. V, 38: on Job 4.18— folly in angls, 20f; VIII, 3, 32; XI, 68; XXII, 15; XXIV: sin and redemption, 147; XXXII, 47: on Ezek. 28.13—orders of angels, 153; XXXIV: identification of Lucifer and Satan, 42.
Gruenbaum, Neue Beiträge, 6; on Kohut's explanation of Aeshma, 85ff; on Shooting Stars, 36.
Guedemann, Das Judentum, 6.

Hadith: definition: Moh. Haggadah, 9.
Haggadah, defined, 1; method of, 3.
Hagigah, 12a: meaning of Shaddai, 2; 12ff: angels praise God, 13.
Halakah, defined, 1.
Halevy, Journal Asiatique, 146ff: on Harut and Marut, 131ff.
Harut and Marut, magic of, 126ff; Moh. angels, 124; versions of story, 134.
Hastings, Dict. Bib.: Whitehouse on name Aeshma, 82.
Haurvatat and Ameratat, 90ff.
Heller, Ch. Jerus. Targum, 118.
Hillel b. Samuel, et al.: on natural exegesis of Bib. angelology, 17.
Hirsch, JQR, new series, vol. XIII: on Is. 14.12: 29.
Hoffman, Dr. David: vs. authority of Hag., 6.

Hulin, 60a: form of Adam, 140.

Iblis: rebellious angel (Moh.), 53–4, 59ff.
Ibn Abbas, 81, 83: on Iblis' rebellion, 60ff.
Ibn Harig: on Koran XXI, 30: 64n.
Irenaeus, I, 2: fall of angels, 121; against heresies, 42 on transmission of tradition, 7.
Isaac of Corbeil: Sepher Miswot Katan, 13.
Isaiah 27.1, et al.: two Leviathan 27; 54.13: interpreted, 3.
Isnad: Moh. chain of authorities, 9; 346: Harut and Marut, 137.

Jastrow, 923b: def. of Nephilim, 115; on Gen. Rab. 8.5: 45.
Jellinek, Bet Hammidrasch II, 115; on Gen. Rab. 8.5: 45.
Jellinek, Bet Hammidrasch II, 39; IV, 27: 49.
Jerome, as Agadist, 161.
Jerusalmi Abodah Zarah 39: punishment of Solomon, 89.
Jer. Berakot 9a: R. Simon b. Johai comm. on Deut. 28.10: 13.
Jer. Sanhedrin 20: punishment of Solomon, 89.
Jesus, accompanied by angels, 19.
Job. 4.18: 18.
John 35.1: on rival God, 31.
Josephus, Antiquities, 1.13: Bene Elohim as men, 118; XVIII: gods and women, 92.
Joshua b. Nun, Rabbi: worship of men, 65.
Jubilees, 5, 4.15, 5.22: angels and women, 95ff.
Judah b. Bathyra, Rabbi, 68; consequences of fall, 74ff.
Justin Martyr, Apol. II, 6: immoral angels, 121; Apol. 27: 43; Dial. cum Tryph., 49; Pro Christ. ad Senat. Roman.: fall of angels, 123.

Kaatz, S., Die muendliche Lehre und ihr Dogma, 7.
Kazwini, ed. Wuestenfeld, 1, 12: Harut and Marut; Iblis, 129ff on nature of angels, Moh., 23.
Ketubot 77a: angel of death and R. Jos. b. Levi, 39.
Kiddushin 40b: on Job 25.2: 14.
Kohut, G. A., on Ashmedai and Aeshma, 81.
Koran, Sura II, 28–31: preeexistence of angels, 52; 38–32: virtue of angels, 16; 32: fall of Iblis, 59; 96: Harut and Marut story, 138–9.
Sura (Koran) VII, 15; XV, 20f; XVIII, 64; XXXVIII: devil's oath, 54 XLI, 161: holiness of man, 64.

Lactantius, De Origine Erroris II, 15: fall of angels, 121–2.
Lange, Genesis, 90: wrong conc. of Satan, 26.
Leviticus Rabba, 18.7: on Is. 14.-12:29; 21: Satan and solar year, 40.
Lucifer: legend: Is. 14.12–16:27. story, 33–34.
Luther: fallen angel concept. not of N. T., 28.

Maimonides: articles of faith, 7.
Martin, Catholic Religion, 7.
Martinus, Pugio Fidei: Lucifer's disobedience, 35.
Matthew 25.41: punishment of devil and his angels, 42.
Me'ilah 14b: virtue of angels, 13.
Menahot 43b: on Al-Tikre, 3.
Meshnevi (Jelalledin Rumi), p. 113: star of Zohra, 139.
Midrash Abkir: preexistence of angels, 48–49; on Shemhazai and Azael, 104.
Midrash Hane'elam, Gen. 6: on Nephilim, 118.
Midrash Haggadah, Gen., 126: R. Berachia on creation of man, 47.
Midrash Psalms, 27.3: no fear of Satan, 40; 82.7: on Is. 14.12: 30.
Midrash Ruth: "Bene Elohim," 118.
Midrash Shem Tob: on Ps. 17.7: 13.
Milton, Paradise Lost, 36.
Mishne Yoma VI, Y: killing of Azazel, 156.
Moses ha-Darshan, Rabbi, 35.
Mujahid: var. of Harut and Marut story, 138.

Nahmanides: on "Bene Elohim," 117; origin of Adam and Eve, 102.
Nephilim, 106; origin, 109; various names, 110.
New Testament: angels elevated and degraded; Acts 7.30, 38; cp. Heb. 2.2: 19.
Numbers Rabba, 9.30: on Is. 14.12: 30; 19: on demons, 32; 19.3: on creation of man, 46.

Onkelos: on "Bene Elohim," 101–2.
Oppert, Exped. de Mesopotamie, I, 178; II, 27ff, 131.
Origen, De Principiis, Pref. 6: devil and his angels, 43.

Palmer, Dr. A. Smythe: shooting stars, 36.
Pesahim, 54a; splendor of Adam, 141; 110a: on Ashmedai, 82.
Pesikta, 108a: virtue of angels, 13n.
Pesikta Rabbeti: seven heavens, 14. II: good angels, 13n; 16: good angels, 13n; 34: on Uza and Azael, 111.
Philo, De Gigantibus: on Gen. 6. 1–4: 17; De Opificio Mundi, 18.
Pirke de R. Eliezer: Torah objects to creation of man, 51; 2: fall of man, 56; 11: creation of man,

47; 11; repentance of Adam, 144; 13: fall of man, 57; 20: Targ. Jon. ad locum; punishment of serpent, 70; 21: Samael and Eve, 78; 22: Bene Elohim, 120ff; 35: on Is. 14.12: 30.
Pseudo-Jonathan: interp. of Bene Elohim, 118.
Pugio Fidei, 563: Satan's fall; refusal to worship Adam, 65; 728: on Bene Elohim, 111–2; Comm. by Zunz, Geiger, Neubauer, Epstein, Gruenbaum, 66–7.
Punishment of Adam and Eve, 72.

Rabbi (Judah), Ha-Nassi the use of the serpent, 69.
Reitzenstein, Poimandres, 228ff, 308ff: gods and women, 92.
Revelation of Moses: punishment of serpent, 72.
Rival god: Persian view, 31.
Rivayet Yasna, 915: fallen angels, 91.
Rosenfeld, M., Der Mid. Deut. Rabba, 13.
Rosenzweig, A., "Die Al-Tikre Deutungen," 2.
Roskoff, Geschichte des Teufels, 181:23.
Ruth Rabba 33: on Is. 14.12: 30.

Samael and Eve, 78; as Satan and serpent, 79; etymology, 80; ident. with Satan, 77.
Samuel Ha-Nagid: vs. authority of Hag., 5.
(Talmud) Sanhedrin 38b: creation of man, 46–47; 38b: yeser hara, angels, 16; 49b: fall of man, 56; 98a: personal Messiah rejected, 4.
Satan: Jewish conception, 37; Moh. story, 34–35; in N. T., 32–33; 42ff; independence and power— John 12.31; Mat. 4; Rom. 16.20; et al., 31; non-existence at creation, 48; O. T.—Job 1.6; Zech. 3.1 et al., 25; oath of revenge, 54ff; other falls, 148; second fall, 56ff; the two—serpent in Gen. and Satan of N. T., 23.
Sayce, Gifford Lects., 1901, pp. 315ff, 361ff, 361f: Bab. parallels of N. T. angels, 19.
Schaff, Creeds of Christendom, 9.
Schatzhoehle (ed. Bezold), p. 5: fall of man, 57; ch. 3, Adam and Jesus, 141–2; ch. 5: Satan Legend, 53; 9: punishment of serpent, 71; III: Satan's deception, 79.
Schechter, Solomon, Aspects, 6.
Schmid, Manual of Patrology, 8.
Schrader, Die Keilinschriften und das A. T., 463ff: the two Satans, 25.
Schwab, Vocab. d'Angelologie, 49.
Serpent and Eve, 69; before fall, 69; gifted with speech, 77; punished, 70.
Septuagint: on fallen angels, 108; on Job, fallen angels, 17.
Shabbat, 32a, et al.: singleness of Satan's power, 39; 55a: imperfect man, 142; 66b: on knowledge of sages, 5; 88b: giving of Torah, 15; 89a: virtue of angels, 13; 146a: sensuality of idolators, 55; 149b: R. Johanan on Is. 14.12: 28.
Sheda (Satan), 58.
Shemhazai and Azael: lust after earth women, 104ff.
Sherira Gaon, Rabbi: vs. authority of Hag., 5.
Sifre, Numb. 42: angels, 13.
Smith, H. P.: Christian Haggadah,
Sofer M., re Dogma p. 79.
Solomon: punishment, 89.
Sons of Seth, 121.
Sotah 9b: on serpent, 69.
Spiegel, Fr., Eran. Altertumskunde, II, 39.40: 91.
Sunna: Moh. Halakah, 9.

Tabari, Hist. I, 78, 166: 59–60. I, 85: 62. I, 80: 63: on Iblis, the Jinn.; I, 85: rebellion of Iblis, 54; I, 169: Iblis and lustful angels, 124ff; I, 340: magic of Harut and Marut, 127; I, 341, 10; 11ff: Harut and Marut, 133; I, 343, 27ff: versions of H. and M. Story, 134; Comm., I, 341, 10;6; 340: 126–7; on Koran II, 28–31:52.
Tanhuma Exodus XXIII: good angels, 13n.
Targum Jer. Genesis 3.6: Samael and the serpent, 78; 4.1: Samael and Eve, 78.
Targum Jon., on Sotah 9b, 70.
Tens, in Jewish lore, 153.
Ten orders: in Talmud, 154–5.
Tertullian: authority of bishops, 7–8.
Tobit: cncerning Ashmedai, 89f.
Tryphon: on "Bene Elohim," 117.

Vendidad III, 24: fall of angels. 90; Fargard XXII, 2–6; XIX: on Angramainyus, the serpent, 40.
Venus, 128–9.
Vita Adae, 13.1: fall of devil, 58–9.

Weber, Jewish Theology, 6.

Wiedemann, Herodot II, 268: gods and women, 92.
Wohlgemuth, Das Juedische Religionsgesetz, 6.

Yalkut, 44: on Aza and Azael, 115.
Yalkut Gen. 25: on Samael, 78.
Yalkut Hadash, 78: Samael as serpent and Satan, 79 on Zohar, Gen. 4.1: 78.
Yasna, 915.46; 40.6; fall of angels, 90.
Yebamoth, 103b: sensuality of idolators, 55.
Yelammedenu: on Numb. XII, 13.
Yezer Hara, 79.
Yoma, 67b: Azazel in folklore, 156; Satan and solar year, 40.

Zecharia, 3.1: Satan accuser of evil, 26: 3.2: 19.
Zendavesta: Angromainyus leaps from heaven as serpent, 24.
Zohar: fallen angels, 103; Gen. 4.1: Samael and Eve, 78 on Yalkut 44: Aza and Azael, 115; 1, 184; 183: Bene Elohim, 119.
Zohra, star of, 139.
Zunz, Gottesdienstliche Vortraege, 13; 311ff, on Yalkut, 78.

www.ingramcontent.com/pod-product-compliance
Lightning Source LLC
Chambersburg PA
CBHW051931160426
43198CB00012B/2114